AIM Higher!

The New Comprehensive English Examination Guide

2nd Edition

by Robert D. Shepherd

Great Source
a division of Houghton Mifflin Harcourt
Wilmington, MA

www.greatsource.com

Staff Credits

Editorial

Diane Perkins Castro

Annie Sun Choi

Sharon S. Salinger

Robert D. Shepherd

Kelsey Stevenson

Production & Design

Matthew Pasquerella

aim higher! More than just teaching to the test™

Second Edition

Printed in the United States of America

12 13   CRW   10 09

International Standard Book Number-13: 1-58171-071-7

Fast Track No: 58171-071-1

NY City Vendor No.: EDU-164

NY City Contract No.: 7000343

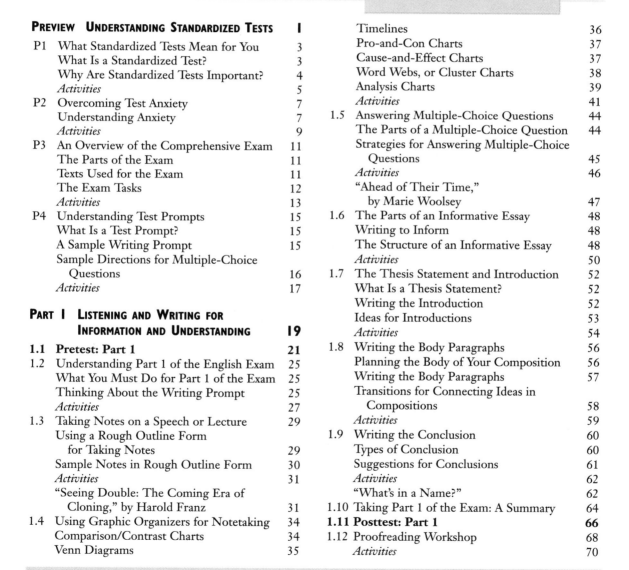

The New Comprehensive English Examination Guide

File   Activity   Edit   Help

Read a Book
See a Movie
Visit a Friend
Prepare for Comp. Exam
Do Some Homework
Listen to CDs

PREVIEW   UNDERSTANDING STANDARDIZED TESTS   1

P1   What Standardized Tests Mean for You   3
    What Is a Standardized Test?   3
    Why Are Standardized Tests Important?   4
    Activities   5
P2   Overcoming Test Anxiety   7
    Understanding Anxiety   7
    Activities   9
P3   An Overview of the Comprehensive Exam   11
    The Parts of the Exam   11
    Texts Used for the Exam   11
    The Exam Tasks   12
    Activities   13
P4   Understanding Test Prompts   15
    What Is a Test Prompt?   15
    A Sample Writing Prompt   15
    Sample Directions for Multiple-Choice
       Questions   16
    Activities   17

**PART 1   LISTENING AND WRITING FOR
           INFORMATION AND UNDERSTANDING   19**

1.1   **Pretest: Part 1**   **21**
1.2   Understanding Part 1 of the English Exam   25
    What You Must Do for Part 1 of the Exam   25
    Thinking About the Writing Prompt   25
    Activities   27
1.3   Taking Notes on a Speech or Lecture   29
    Using a Rough Outline Form
       for Taking Notes   29
    Sample Notes in Rough Outline Form   30
    Activities   31
    "Seeing Double: The Coming Era of
       Cloning," by Harold Franz   31
1.4   Using Graphic Organizers for Notetaking   34
    Comparison/Contrast Charts   34
    Venn Diagrams   35

    Timelines   36
    Pro-and-Con Charts   37
    Cause-and-Effect Charts   37
    Word Webs, or Cluster Charts   38
    Analysis Charts   39
    Activities   41
1.5   Answering Multiple-Choice Questions   44
    The Parts of a Multiple-Choice Question   44
    Strategies for Answering Multiple-Choice
       Questions   45
    Activities   46
    "Ahead of Their Time,"
       by Marie Woolsey   47
1.6   The Parts of an Informative Essay   48
    Writing to Inform   48
    The Structure of an Informative Essay   48
    Activities   50
1.7   The Thesis Statement and Introduction   52
    What Is a Thesis Statement?   52
    Writing the Introduction   52
    Ideas for Introductions   53
    Activities   54
1.8   Writing the Body Paragraphs   56
    Planning the Body of Your Composition   56
    Writing the Body Paragraphs   57
    Transitions for Connecting Ideas in
       Compositions   58
    Activities   59
1.9   Writing the Conclusion   60
    Types of Conclusion   60
    Suggestions for Conclusions   61
    Activities   62
    "What's in a Name?"   62
1.10   Taking Part 1 of the Exam: A Summary   64
1.11   **Posttest: Part 1**   **66**
1.12   Proofreading Workshop   68
    Activities   70

PART 2 READING AND WRITING FOR INFORMATION AND UNDERSTANDING   71

2.1 **Pretest: Part 2**   73
"Our Place on the Planet: Biodiversity and Human Ends,"
by Dr. Héctor A. Sánchez   75
2.2 Understanding Part 2 of the English Exam   79
What You Must Do for Part 2 of the Exam   79
Thinking About the Writing Prompt   79
Activities   81
2.3 Distinguishing Facts and Opinions   83
Fact or Opinion?   83
Proving Facts   84
Types of Opinion   84
Supporting Opinions   85
Understanding Facts and Opinions   86
Activities   87
2.4 Organizing Ideas Using Facts and Opinions   89
Persuasive and Informative Writing   89
Organizing Persuasive and Informative Writing   89
Activities   91
2.5 Analyzing Infographics   93
Visual Materials on Part 2 of the Examination   93
Understanding Line Graphs   93
Understanding Bar Graphs   95
Understanding Column Graphs   95
Understanding Pie Charts   96
Understanding Tables   98
Other Visual Materials: Diagrams, Plots, and Maps   99
Analyzing an Informational Graphic   101
Activities   102
2.6 Taking Part 2 of the Exam: A Summary   106
2.7 **Posttest: Part 2**   108
"Economic Report Card Shows Continued Inequity," by Elizabeth Brinkman   109
2.8 Proofreading Workshop   112

PART 3 READING AND WRITING FOR LITERARY RESPONSE   113

3.1 **Pretest: Part 3**   115
"Death, Be Not Proud," by John Donne   117
from "The Death of Iván Illych," by Leo Tolstoy   118
3.2 Understanding Part 3 of the English Exam   122
What You Must Do for Part 3 of the Exam   122
Thinking About the Writing Prompt   122
Activities   124
3.3 Literary Genres, Elements, and Techniques   126
Genres of Literature   126
Types of Prose Narrative   126
Types of Poem   127
Literary Elements and Techniques   128
Elements and Techniques Found in All Genres of Literature   128
Figurative Language   129
Rhetorical Techniques   130
Techniques Involving Sound   130
"A Birthday," by Christina Rossetti   130
Some Literary Elements Peculiar to Poetry   131
Activities   132
3.4 Reading a Lyric Poem   133
Steps in Reading a Lyric Poem   133
"Have You Forgotten?" by James Worley   133
Taking Notes on a Poem During the Exam   136
"Brahma," by Ralph Waldo Emerson   138
"Alone," by Edgar Allan Poe   139
Activities   140
3.5 Reading a Narrative   141
Understanding Narratives   141
"The Story of an Hour," by Kate Chopin   141
The Elements of a Narrative   145
Taking Notes on a Narrative During the Exam   146
Activities   148
3.6 Using Quotations as Evidence in Your Writing   153
Quoting Versus Paraphrasing or Summarizing   153
Guidelines for Quoting   154
Activities   156
3.7 Outlining a Composition to Contrast Literary Works   157
Essays That Contrast   157
Organizing an Essay That Contrasts   157
Activities   159
3.8 Taking Part 3 of the Exam: A Summary   160
3.9 **Posttest: Part 3**   162
3.10 Proofreading Workshop   165

PART 4 READING AND WRITING FOR CRITICAL ANALYSIS AND EVALUATION 167

4.1 **Pretest: Part 4** 169
4.2 Understanding Part 4 of the English Exam 171
What You Must Do for Part 4 of the Exam 171
Thinking About the Writing Prompt 171
Activities 174
4.3 Analyzing Critical Lens Statements 176
Defining the Critical Lens Statement 176
Understanding the Critical Lens Statement 176
Formulating a Thesis Statement 177
Sample Critical Lens Statements 178
Activities 179
4.4 Prior Preparation for Part 4 of the Exam 180
Preparing for Part 4 of the Exam 180
Choosing Works to Study for the Exam 182
Activities 183
4.5 Writing Your Essay for Part 4 of the Exam 184
Activities 186
4.6 Taking Part 4 of the Exam: A Summary 187
4.7 **Posttest: Part 4** 188

PART 5 COMPLETE PRACTICE TEST 189

Complete Practice Test: Session 1 191
Part 1: Listening and Writing for Information and Understanding 192
Part 2: Reading and Writing for Information and Understanding 194

Complete Practice Test: Session 2 199
Part 3: Reading and Writing for Literary Response 200
Part 4: Reading and Writing for Critical Analysis and Evaluation 206

APPENDICES 207

A. Multiple-Choice Answer Sheet 207
B. Proofreading Checklist 208
C. The Organization of a Five-Paragraph Theme 209
D. Commonly Misspelled Words 210
E. Vocabulary Used in Examination Prompts 213
F. Vocabulary Used to Describe Genres and Parts of Writing and Literature 216

LISTENING SELECTIONS FOR PRETESTS AND POSTTESTS, LESSON 1.4, AND COMPLETE PRACTICE TEST 221

INDEX 231

LITERARY AND NONFICTION WORKS IN THIS EDITION

"Seeing Double: The Coming Era of Cloning," by Harold Franz (article) 31

"Ahead of Their Time," by Marie Woolsey (article) 47

"What's in a Name?" by R. Pasteur (essay) 62

"Our Place on the Planet: Biodiversity and Human Ends," by Dr. Héctor A. Sánchez (magazine article) 75

"Economic Report Card Shows Continued Inequity," by Elizabeth Brinkman (newspaper article) 109

"Death, Be Not Proud," by John Donne (poem) 117

from "The Death of Iván Illych," by Leo Tolstoy, trans. by Robin Lamb (short story) 118

"A Birthday," by Christina Rossetti (poem) 130

"Have You Forgotten?" by James Worley (poem) 133

"Brahma," by Ralph Waldo Emerson (poem) 138

"Alone," by Edgar Allan Poe (poem) 139

"The Story of an Hour," by Kate Chopin (short story) 141

"Old Saying, New Meaning: Everything in Moderation," by Anita Shriver (magazine article) 195

"Boast Not, Proud English," by Roger Williams (poem) 201

from "Remarks Concerning the Natives of North America," by Benjamin Franklin (essay) 202

"The Birth of the Net," from *The Complete Student's Guide to the Internet*, by Allyson Stanford (nonfiction) 221

"Careers for Art Students," by Ellen Best (essay) 223

from "All the Pretty Little Ponies," by Jo Dignee (short story) 224

"A Talent for Turning It Around," by Yvonne Barett (biographical essay) 224

from *They Fought for Freedom*, by Dale Berger (biographical essay) 226

"Pompeii: the Time Machine," by Robin Shulka (lecture) 228

To
Ada,
Alex,
Brittany,
Kai,
Myles, &
Robin

The Future

Preview:

Understanding
Standardized Tests

The number 1 rule of test-taking is "Don't panic." The number 2 rule is "Be prepared." Study the lessons in this book, answer the study questions, and take the practice tests. Doing so will enable you to face the examination with confidence.

Lesson P.1

What Standardized Tests Mean for You

See Movie
Call Friend
Listen to CDs
Read Lesson P.1
Go to Concert
Go Shopping

What Is a Standardized Test?

During World War I, the people who ran the United States armed services had a problem. They needed to figure out which of their new soldiers would make the best officers. They could easily tell, from what they were doing in basic training, which young recruits were the strongest, which were best at taking orders, which could hold up under pressure, and so on. They needed to know more, however. In particular, they needed to know which soldiers were bright enough to become officers charged with making decisions and solving problems. So, they created the first standardized tests taken by large numbers of Americans. A **standardized test** is one that is given to many people to compare their abilities or to compare what they have learned.[1] There are two types of standardized test: the aptitude test and the achievement test.

 Two Types of Standardized Test

1. An **aptitude test** tells what general abilities a person has. It isn't supposed to measure anything particular that a person has learned. Instead, it tells how capable someone is of learning. For example, an aptitude test for typing might measure how quickly and carefully you can move your fingers and whether you can read—two basic skills that typists have to have. Someone who could move his or her fingers very quickly and carefully might have a lot of **aptitude,** or general ability, for learning to type. IQ tests are one kind of aptitude test. They supposedly measure a person's general intelligence—how carefully, clearly, and quickly he or she can think.

---

[1] **standardized test.** Technically, a standardized test is one that has been developed using statistical methods to establish norms for responses to the test questions. In popular usage, a standardized test is any widely used exam of set format. The technical term for a test, like the English Regents, that is correlated to standards or benchmarks is *criterion-referenced examination.*

GUM: Do not ask for (who, whom) the bell tolls.

2. An **achievement test** tells what someone has already learned in some area. For example, after studying typing for a year, you might take an achievement test to find out how fast you can now type. The **Comprehensive Examination in English** is an achievement test that measures what you have learned about listening, reading, writing, and such study skills as taking notes and reading charts and graphs. The purpose of the test is to find out if you have learned enough in these areas to be qualified to receive a high-school diploma. You will learn a lot more about the Comprehensive Examination in English in later lessons. For now, the most important thing for you to understand is that **you will have to pass the Comprehensive Exam in order to graduate from high school.** Don't worry, however. If you work hard and do all the lessons in this book, you shouldn't have any problem passing this test. An achievement test measures what you have learned. So, if you apply yourself and have a positive attitude, you're bound to learn enough to pass the test with flying colors!

Why Are Standardized Tests Important?

Throughout your life, you will take many standardized tests. You already know that you will have to pass the Comprehensive Examination to graduate from high school. If you plan to go to college, you will need to take the **Scholastic Aptitude Test, or SAT.** If you plan, instead, to take a job, you will often find standardized tests there, too. For example, if you want to do office work for a living, you may have to take tests that measure such skills as typing ability or ability to answer the telephone using proper grammar, a clear speaking voice, and polite words and phrases. If you want to sell real estate, to do electrical work or plumbing, or to repair or install computers and computer networks, you will have to take standardized tests to become licensed or certified to do those jobs. Many states now require automobile mechanics to take standardized tests as well. Professionals, such as accountants, therapists, social workers, doctors, medical assistants, pharmacists, and lawyers, have to pass standardized tests before they are allowed to practice. Even dating services sometimes use standardized tests to match people with others who are like them!

The ability to take tests well is a skill that can be learned. Learning this skill can help you throughout your life, making it easier for you to fulfill your dreams. Studying the lessons in this book will help you not only to pass the Comprehensive Examination in English but also the other tests that you will face throughout your life.

ANSWER: whom

File   Activity   Edit   Help

See Movie
Call Friend
Listen to CDs
Do Activities, Lesson P.1
Go to Concert
Go Shopping

A. Recalling the Lesson

Number your paper from 1 to 5. Write the letter of the best answer to each question.

1. **Standardized tests were first given to large numbers of Americans by**
   (a) colleges and universities.
   (b) the Peace Corps.
   (c) accountants, doctors, and lawyers.
   (d) the armed services.

2. **A test that measures a person's ability to learn to type is an example of an**
   (a) aptitude test.
   (b) achievement test.
   (c) oral examination.
   (d) IQ test.

3. **A test given at the end of a typing class to find out how much a person has learned is an example of an**
   (a) aptitude test.
   (b) achievement test.
   (c) oral examination.
   (d) IQ test.

4. **The Comprehensive Examination in English is an example of an**
   (a) aptitude test.
   (b) achievement test.
   (c) oral examination.
   (d) IQ test.

VOC: Words with the root *spec*, meaning "to see"   What Standardized Tests Mean for You   5

5. **A standardized test that people need to take if they plan to go to college is the**
   (a) Graduate Record Examination, or GRE.
   (b) Bar Exam.
   (c) Scholastic Aptitude Test, or SAT.
   (d) Graduate Management Admissions Test, or GMAT.

B. What's Your Aptitude?

No two people are exactly the same. Every person has unique abilities. Number your paper from 1 to 4. Then, on the paper, list four things that you do well—four aptitudes that you have.

Next think about the aptitudes that you listed. Given these aptitudes, what job or career do you think you might be best at in later life? On your own paper, write a paragraph explaining what job or career you think you might be good at and why.

C. Thinking About Your Achievements

An achievement is something that you have learned or something that you have accomplished. Number your paper from 1 to 4. Then list four achievements of which you are particularly proud. These may be as simple as having learned how to skateboard or as complicated as having mastered a computer program.

Next, write a paragraph that tells about one achievement that you would like to accomplish in your adult life. In the body of the paragraph, describe this achievement and tell why it is important to you.

D. Relating Aptitudes to Achievements

Number your paper from 1 to 5. On your paper, list an aptitude that would help to make possible each achievement listed below.

1. **writing an outstanding computer program**

2. **playing left field on a college baseball team**

3. **getting a job as a piano tuner**

4. **getting a job designing windows for a fancy department store**

5. **having lots of friends**

ANSWER: speculate, spectacle, specter, spectator

Lesson P.2
Overcoming Test Anxiety

See Movie
Call Friend
Listen to CDs
Read Lesson P.2
Go to Concert
Go Shopping

Understanding Anxiety

Anxiety is a feeling of uneasiness or worry. People naturally feel anxiety when confronted by new challenges or unknown situations. A little anxiety can be a good thing. It can help to focus a person's attention and make a person alert and ready to act in ways that will bring about positive outcomes. Too much anxiety, however, can be negative. Consider the example of Joel, who plays guitar in a band:

> We had a great gig on New Year's Eve, playing a party that this business-woman was having for her employees. I was really looking forward to it. We got to her place out on Long Island and set up all the equipment. I was tuning up and testing the microphones when our drummer, Nick, told me that this girl I know, Kerrie, was going to be there. It seems her father worked for the woman throwing the party! Sure enough, in walks Kerrie, and all of a sudden, I lost it. When we started to play, I couldn't remember the opening lead riff, and then I forgot some of the words, and it was just a mess.

As this example shows, one of the reasons that people feel anxiety is fear of failure. Joel didn't want to sound bad in front of Kerrie, so he started to feel anxious. Then, his anxiety kept him from performing as well as he usually does.

Many people feel anxious when they are called on to perform in front of an audience—to give a speech, to act in a drama, or to play in a game with spectators watching. People also often feel anxious about performing well on tests. Nervousness, shaking, lack of concentration, negative thoughts, and an inability to remember things one knows well are all signs of such anxiety. Unfortunately, anxiety about tests can actually cause people to do badly on them.

GUM: Let's keep this between you and (I, me).

Dealing with Anxiety

Fortunately, there are ways to deal with anxiety so that it won't negatively affect your performance. If you are anxious about performing well on the Comprehensive Examination in English, combat your anxiety by taking the following steps:

 Combating Test Anxiety

1. **Think Positively.** Negative thoughts can cause people to fail. Before a test, try to think positively about the outcome. Expect that you will succeed, and the chances are much better that in fact you will succeed. Tell yourself, "I am a smart and capable person, and I can do well on this exam."

2. **Prepare Yourself.** The most important thing you can do to combat anxiety is to be prepared for the test. If you are prepared, then you will do well on the test and have nothing to fear. The best way to prepare for the test is to do all the lessons in this book. If you do these lessons, you will know what to expect on the exam, and so it won't be so frightening. In fact, by the time you get to the end of this book, you might even be looking forward to taking the test to show off what you've learned!

3. **Sleep and Eat Well Before the Test.** Whenever you take a test, it is very important that you get plenty of sleep the night before. You should also eat good, nutritious meals the night before and the morning of the exam. Doing these things will help to ensure that you are in peak condition during the exam.

4. **Practice Relaxation Techniques.** If you are very nervous just before the exam, try breathing slowly and deeply a few times. This will help to calm you down. You might also try closing your eyes for a bit and imagining a peaceful, quiet scene.

5. **Don't Be Thrown by Something That You Don't Understand.** Remember that no one is expected to get a perfect score on the exam and that there will be a few things on every test that most people will not understand. When you come across something you don't understand, remain calm, read that part of the exam again carefully, and try to figure out what is being said using context clues. **Context clues** are hints provided by the surrounding text.

6. **Remember That You Can Try Again.** Do not think of the test as your one shot at success. If you do not pass the test on the first try, you can, of course, try again.

ANSWER: me

File   Activity   Edit   Help

See Movie
Call Friend
Listen to CDs
Do Activities, Lesson P.2
Go to Concert
Go Shopping

A. Recalling the Lesson

Number your paper from 1 to 5. Write the letter of the best answer to each question.

1. **Anxiety is**
   (a) a feeling of uneasiness or worry about something that might happen in the future.
   (b) anger about having to do something that one doesn't want to do.
   (c) fear of physical harm.
   (d) a feeling of confidence.

2. **The anxiety that the guitarist Joel felt when he started to play was due to the fact that he**
   (a) couldn't remember the words to a song.
   (b) hadn't practiced enough before playing.
   (c) knew someone in the audience.
   (d) didn't like the kind of music that the band had to play that night.

3. **Giving a speech, acting in a drama, playing a game in front of spectators, and taking tests are all situations in which people commonly feel**
   (a) depressed.
   (b) anxious.
   (c) angry.
   (d) nothing at all.

4. **Signs of anxiety include**
   (a) nervousness and sweating.
   (b) shaking and lack of concentration.
   (c) negative thoughts and memory failure.
   (d) all of the above.

5. **The most valuable thing that a person can do to combat test anxiety is**
   (a) not to think much about the test.
   (b) to prepare well for the test.
   (c) to take the test at another time.
   (d) to ignore the parts of the test that are confusing.

B. Visualizing Success

One secret of successful people in all fields is confidence. Confident people are not crippled by anxiety. They are able to go into a new situation sure that they will be able to succeed. One way to build your confidence about taking the Comprehensive Exam is to visualize yourself taking the exam and doing well on it.

Try this experiment: Imagine that you have just finished taking the Comprehensive Exam and have done extremely well on it. On your own paper, write a short journal entry, dated sometime after the exam, in which you describe taking it. Imagine that on the days of the exam you felt relaxed and confident. As you looked over the exam questions, your confidence grew even more, for you had studied your preparation lessons and knew exactly what to do. After the exam, you were able to tell friends and family members that you thought you did well. Describe these events in your journal entry.

ANSWER: preface, predetermine, prepaid, prenatal

Lesson P.3

An Overview of the Comprehensive Exam

See Movie
Call Friend
Listen to CDs
Read Lesson P.3
Go to Concert
Go Shopping

The Parts of the Exam

The New Comprehensive Examination in English contains four parts, as follows:

Parts of the Exam

Part 1	Listening and Writing for Information and Understanding
Part 2	Reading and Writing for Information and Understanding
Part 3	Reading and Writing for Literary Response
Part 4	Reading and Writing for Critical Analysis and Evaluation

Texts Used for the Exam

In each part of the exam, you will respond to questions about one or more texts. A **text** is a piece of written material. The texts that you will use are as follows:

Texts Used for Each Part of the Exam

Text, Part 1	A listening passage that is read aloud to you
Texts, Part 2	An informative article with one or more visuals, such as charts, graphs, tables, diagrams, maps, or illustrations, to interpret
Texts, Part 3	Two or more short literary works (for example, a poem and a selection from a diary)
Texts, Part 4	Two literary works that you have read previously

Notice that for Parts 1, 2, and 3 of the exam, you will be responding to short texts that you probably have not seen or heard before. You will listen to, read, study, and take notes on these texts during the exam. For Part 4 of the exam, you will respond to a writing assignment by referring to texts that you have previously read.

GUM: There isn't (anything, nothing) to worry about.

The Exam Tasks

For Part 4 of the exam, you will have a single **task** to perform: you will create an extended written response based on texts that you have read before. An extended written response is a piece of writing several paragraphs long.

For each of the other parts of the exam, you will have two tasks to perform. You will answer a set of multiple-choice questions based on the text(s). Then you will do an extended piece of writing based on the text(s).

The following chart summarizes the exam tasks for each part.

Tasks for Each Part of the Exam

Part 1 Listening and Writing for Information and Understanding
Task 1: Answer multiple-choice questions about the listening passage
Task 2: Write an extended written response to the listening passage

Part 2 Reading and Writing for Information and Understanding
Task 1: Answer multiple-choice questions about the informative reading and the visual materials, such as tables, charts, and graphs
Task 2: Write an extended written response to the informative reading and to the visual materials

Part 3 Reading and Writing for Literary Response
Task 1: Answer multiple-choice questions about the short literary works
Task 2: Write an extended written response to the short literary works

Part 4 Reading and Writing for Critical Analysis and Evaluation
Task: Write an extended written response based on literature you have read previously

To be successful on the Comprehensive Exam, you will have to be able to listen and read for information, interpret visual materials, interpret literary works, take notes, answer multiple-choice questions, and respond in writing to various kinds of text. The lessons in this book will help you to develop these skills.

ANSWER: anything

File   Activity   Edit   Help

    See Movie
    Call Friend
    Listen to CDs
    Do Activities, Lesson P.3
    Go to Concert
    Go Shopping

 Recalling the Lesson

Number your paper from 1 to 5. Write the letter of the best answer to each question.

1. The part of the exam in which you respond to a listening passage is
   (a) Part 1.
   (b) Part 2.
   (c) Part 3.
   (d) Part 4.

2. The only part of the exam that does not have a multiple-choice task is
   (a) Part 1.
   (b) Part 2.
   (c) Part 3.
   (d) Part 4.

3. The written responses that you do for each part of the exam must all
   (a) be several paragraphs long.
   (b) deal with literary works that you have studied in class.
   (c) deal with literary works that are given to you with the exam.
   (d) include visual materials, such as tables, charts, and graphs.

4. The part of the exam that deals with short literary works is
   (a) Part 1.
   (b) Part 2.
   (c) Part 3.
   (d) Part 4.

5. To be successful on Part 4 of the exam, you will have to
   (a) take careful notes on the listening passage.
   (b) read and study several literary works before you take the test.
   (c) understand how to interpret tables, charts, and graphs.
   (d) read and study two literary works that you are given with the exam.

B. Creating a Chart

Copy the following chart onto a piece of paper and fill it in using information presented in the lesson.

Parts, Texts, and Tasks on the Comprehensive Examination

Part No.	Name of Part	Text(s) Used	Task(s) Required
1			
2			
3			
4			

ANSWER: democracy, democrat, demographer

Lesson P.4

Understanding Test Prompts

See Movie
Call Friend
Listen to CDs
Read Lesson P.4
Go to Concert
Go Shopping

What Is a Test Prompt?

A **test prompt** is a set of information and directions telling you what to do for a part of a test. The Comprehensive Examination in English contains two kinds of test prompt—**writing prompts** and **directions for multiple-choice questions.** In later lessons in this book, you will see many examples of the specific kinds of prompt that appear on the Comprehensive Exam. In this lesson, you will learn about the two kinds of prompt that are on the exam.

A Sample Writing Prompt

The writing prompt for Part 1 of the Comprehensive Exam has three parts: **Overview,** or **Directions; The Situation;** and **Your Task.** The writing prompt below is an example, provided for analysis. Do not actually carry out the directions given in the prompt.

Overview: For this part of the test, you will listen to a lecture about the history of the exploration of Mars and then write a response based on the situation described below. You will also answer some multiple-choice questions about key ideas in the lecture.

The Situation: As part of your summer job at a science museum, your responsibility is to help visiting high-school students understand and appreciate a new exhibit called "The Red Planet." The exhibit contains posters, photographs, machines, and other materials related to the history of the exploration of Mars. To prepare for your role, your supervisor has asked you to attend a lecture about Mars exploration. Then you will use information from the lecture to write an essay that will appear in a guide to be given to high-school students viewing the exhibit.

GUM: Please (accept, except) this small gift.

You will hear the lecture twice. You may take notes on the sheet provided at any time during the readings.

Your Task: Write the essay on Mars Exploration to be included in the visitors' guide.

Guidelines:
Be sure to:

- Provide your audience with background information that will help them to understand and appreciate the exhibit
- Use accurate, specific information from the lecture
- Organize your ideas in a unified and coherent manner
- Follow the conventions of standard written English

The writing prompt asks you to imagine a real-life situation in which you might be called on to listen and then respond in writing. It provides the following information:

- Source: where you will get the information for your writing
- Topic: what you will be writing about
- Form: what kind of piece you will be writing (story, essay, letter, etc.)
- Audience: those for whom you will be writing
- Purpose: why you are writing and what the piece of writing should accomplish

Sample Directions for Multiple-Choice Questions

The directions for multiple-choice questions in the Comprehensive Exam look something like this:

Directions: Use your notes to answer the following questions about the lecture. Select the word or expression that best answers each question. The questions may help you think about ideas and information from the lecture that you might want to use in your visitors' guide essay.

ANSWER: accept

File   Activity   Edit   Help

See Movie
Call Friend
Listen to CDs
Do Activities, Lesson P.4
Go to Concert
Go Shopping

Recalling the Lesson

Number your paper from 1 to 5. Write the letter of the best answer to each question.

1. A set of information and directions that tells what to do on an exam is
   (a)   a discussion question.
   (b)   an exercise.
   (c)   a test prompt.
   (d)   a multiple-choice question.

2. After reading a writing prompt, you should be able to identify
   (a)   your audience.
   (b)   your purpose.
   (c)   your topic.
   (d)   all of the above.

3. The part of the Comprehensive Exam writing prompt that contains a bulleted list of goals that you must meet in your writing is called
   (a)   Overview or Directions.
   (b)   The Situation.
   (c)   Your Task.
   (d)   none of the above.

4. The form of a piece of writing is
   (a)   where you will get the information that you will be writing about.
   (b)   those for whom you will be writing.
   (c)   what you will be writing about.
   (d)   what kind of piece you will be writing (essay, letter, etc.).

5. The Comprehensive Examination in English contains
   (a)   one kind of test prompt.
   (b)   two kinds of test prompt.
   (c)   three kinds of test prompt.
   (d)   four kinds of test prompt.

VOC: Words with the prefix *mal–*, meaning "bad"

B. Analyzing the Prompts

Study the two test prompts given in the lesson. Then, on your own paper, answer the following questions. Questions 1–9 refer to the writing prompt.

1. **Source:** From what source is the student supposed to get his or her information? What does the student need to do to gather this information from the source?

2. **Topic:** About what topic is the student supposed to write?

3. **Form:** What kind of piece of writing is the student supposed to do? Do you expect that the piece of writing should have more than one paragraph? Why, or why not?

4. **Audience:** For whom is the student supposed to write? In other words, who is the intended audience for the piece?

5. **Purpose:** What is the overall purpose of this piece of writing?

6. **Goals:** What four specific goals must the student meet in the piece of writing that he or she does in response to this prompt?

7. **Organization:** The writing prompt says that the piece of writing is supposed to be "organized in a unified and coherent manner." Look up the terms *unified* and *coherent* in a dictionary. What do these terms mean? What makes a unified and coherent piece of writing different from one that isn't unified and coherent?

8. **Development:** The writing prompt says that the piece of writing should be developed using "accurate, specific information." What is accurate information? What is specific information?

9. **Conventions:** The writing prompt says that the writer should "follow the conventions of standard written English." What is a convention? What is standard written English? What are some examples of nonstandard written English?

10. **The Multiple-Choice Prompt:** This prompt tells the student to "select the word or expression that best answers each question." What is an expression? How does it differ from a word? How might answering the multiple-choice questions help the student to write his or her visitor's guide essay?

C. Group Project

Working with several other students, review the writing prompt and make a complete list, in order, of everything that a person would have to do to respond properly to this prompt.

ANSWER: maladjusted, malcontent, malfunction

Part 1

Listening and Writing for Information and Understanding

19

Hearing is not the same as listening. Listening requires much, much more—engagement, attention, analysis, and understanding. Animals can hear. It takes a particularly intelligent human being to listen.

Lesson 1.1

Pretest: Part 1

See Movie
Call Friend
Listen to CDs
Take Pretest: Part 1
Go to Concert
Go Shopping

The test booklet for Part 1 of the Comprehensive English Examination will look similar to what you find in this lesson. Take this Pretest as if you were taking the actual exam.

HIGH SCHOOL

COMPREHENSIVE EXAMINATION

IN

ENGLISH

PART 1

This part of the examination tests listening skills. You are to listen as a selection is read, answer twenty multiple-choice questions about it, and write a response, as directed. On page 207 of this book, you will find a sample answer sheet for the multiple-choice questions. To take the test in this book, you will use your own paper to answer the multiple-choice questions and write your essay.

DO NOT TURN THE PAGE UNTIL THE SIGNAL IS GIVEN.

GUM: (She, Her) and Yolanda are writing a screenplay.

Part 1: Listening and Writing for Information and Understanding

Overview: For this part of the test, you will listen to a lecture about the Internet and answer some multiple-choice questions about key ideas in the lecture. Then you will write a response based on the situation described below. You will hear the lecture twice. You may take notes on a separate piece of paper at any time you wish during the readings.

The Situation: You have taken a summer job working for a local computer museum in its Internet Education Program. This program trains high-school students to use the Internet for research. Your supervisor, the director of the Internet Education Program, has asked you to write a guide called "A Brief History of the Internet" to be given to high-school students entering the Internet Education Program. In preparation for writing your article, listen to a speech given by writer Allyson Stanford. Then use relevant information from the speech to write your article.

Your Task: Write a "Brief History of the Internet" to be given to high-school students to provide them with background information on what the Internet and the World Wide Web are and how they were developed.

Guidelines:

Be sure to

- Explain to your audience what the Internet and the World Wide Web are and how they were developed
- Use accurate, specific information from the lecture
- Organize your ideas in a unified and coherent manner
- Follow the conventions of standard written English

ANSWER: She

Multiple-Choice Questions

Directions: Use your notes to answer the following questions about the lecture. Select the best answer and write its letter on your answer sheet. The questions may help you think of ideas from the lecture to use in your writing. You may return to these questions any time you wish.

1. **The Internet is a**
   (a) large system of interconnected computers that spans the globe.
   (b) kind of software used to connect computers.
   (c) defense department computer.
   (d) service that sells connection time to computer users.

2. **Computers can be connected to the Internet by means of**
   (a) telephone lines.
   (b) cables like those used for cable television.
   (c) wireless connections.
   (d) all of the above.

3. **The Advanced Research Projects Agency was created by**
   (a) Dr. Tim Berners-Lee.
   (b) President Jimmy Carter.
   (c) President George Bush.
   (d) none of the above.

4. **The network that evolved into the modern-day Internet was known as**
   (a) the Military Network.
   (b) ARPANet.
   (c) CompuServe.
   (d) America Online.

5. **People started using the term *Internet* to describe the worldwide system of connected computers in the early**
   (a) 1960s.
   (b) 1970s.
   (c) 1980s.
   (d) 1990s.

6. **The inventor of the part of the Internet known as the World Wide Web was**
   (a) Tim Berners-Lee.
   (b) Dwight D. Eisenhower.
   (c) Marvin Minsky.
   (d) Al Gore.

7. **The Internet was given a peer-to-peer structure instead of a centralized structure so that parts of it would**
   (a) be more powerful than any computer ever built.
   (b) last into the twenty-first century.
   (c) survive bombing during a war.
   (d) be useful for doing research papers.

8. **The early Internet was**
   (a) text based.
   (b) graphics based.
   (c) movie based.
   (d) none of the above.

9. **Pages on the World Wide Web**
   (a) were first created by President Dwight D. Eisenhower.
   (b) are stored on computers at the Department of Defense.
   (c) can include only text.
   (d) can include not only text but also pictures, sound, and video.

10. **What makes the World Wide Web special is that pages around the world are connected by means of**
    (a) tables.
    (b) charts.
    (c) links.
    (d) paper clips.

GUM: (Who's, Whose) idea was that?

Pretest: Part I   23

Copyrighted material. Not to be photocopied.

11. **Another name for the Internet is**
    (a) the Advanced Research Projects Agency.
    (b) the World Wide Web.
    (c) the Information Superhighway.
    (d) CERN.

12. **Allyson Stanford predicts that one consequence of connecting the entire world will be that the differences between the haves and the have-nots will**
    (a) increase.
    (b) decrease.
    (c) disappear.
    (d) remain the same.

13. **A person can use the Internet to**
    (a) do research.
    (b) do shopping.
    (c) send electronic mail, or e-mail.
    (d) all of the above.

14. **Most people connect to the Internet from**
    (a) personal computers.
    (b) mainframe computers.
    (c) workstations.
    (d) all of the above.

15. **Pages on the World Wide Web can contain not only text but also**
    (a) pictures.
    (b) sound.
    (c) movies.
    (d) all of the above.

16. **What was the main purpose of the ARPANet?**
    (a) to connect scientific researchers
    (b) to enable people to do online shopping
    (c) to replace television with online movies
    (d) to warn ordinary Americans about missile attacks

17. **To click on a link in a World Wide Web page, a person uses a**
    (a) modem.
    (b) telephone line.
    (c) workstation.
    (d) mouse.

18. **The World Wide Web is part of**
    (a) the ARPANet.
    (b) the Internet.
    (c) electronic mail, or e-mail.
    (d) the Military Defense Network.

19. **A _____ is a computer on which World Wide Web pages are stored.**
    (a) mainframe
    (b) personal computer
    (c) workstation
    (d) server

20. **One use of the World Wide Web not mentioned in the reading is to**
    (a) do shopping.
    (b) pay bills.
    (c) do videoconferencing.
    (d) send electronic mail.

ANSWER: Whose

Lesson 1.2

Understanding Part I of the English Exam

See Movie
Call Friend
Listen to CDs
Read Lesson 1.2
Go to Concert
Go Shopping

What You Must Do for Part I of the Exam

As you saw when you took the Pretest, Part 1 of the New Comprehensive Examination in English requires you to do the following:

1. Listen to a reading

2. Take notes as you listen

3. Answer some multiple-choice questions about the reading

4. Do a piece of writing based on the reading

Thinking About the Writing Prompt

In the lessons that follow, you will learn how to listen carefully to a reading or lecture, how to take notes as you listen, and how to answer multiple-choice questions. For now, we shall concentrate on understanding the parts of the writing prompt. Before continuing with this lesson, go back and reread the writing prompt given on page 22. The writing prompt provides a great deal of information about the piece of writing that is to be done, as follows:

- **Source.** The prompt tells you that the information for the piece of writing will come from notes that you take on the reading. Therefore, it will be important to take good notes.

- **Topic.** The prompt tells you that your topic will be the history of the Internet.

- **Form.** The prompt tells you that you will be writing a guide for high-school students. Notice that the prompt does not tell you, exactly, how many paragraphs you need to write. For each part of the Comprehensive Examination, unless you are specifically told in the directions to do otherwise, make sure that you write at least five paragraphs.

GUM: (Their, There) are two concert tickets left.

- **Audience.** The audience for the piece of writing will be other high-school students (those who are going to participate in the museum's Internet program).

- **Purpose.** The purpose of the paragraph is to provide information. In other words, this is to be an informative composition. The Your Task section of the writing prompt explains two purposes that the answer must accomplish. First, the composition must explain what the Internet and the World Wide Web are. Second, the composition must tell how the Internet and the World Wide Web were developed.

- **Organization.** The writing prompt does not tell you, exactly, how to organize your composition. However, since you are to write about the history of the Internet, you will probably want to organize the composition in **chronological order,** or time order. The Your Task section of the writing prompt tells you that the composition should be organized in a "unified and coherent manner." A piece of writing is **organized** if the order of its ideas makes sense. A piece of writing is **unified** if its ideas all relate to the thesis or controlling purpose. It is **coherent** if its ideas are connected to one another in ways that show the logical relationships among them. One way to connect ideas is to use transitions. **Transitions** are words and phrases like *first, therefore, in addition, furthermore, later,* and *in conclusion* that connect ideas.

- **Development.** The Your Task section of the writing prompt says that you should develop your piece of writing using specific, accurate information from the reading.

- **Conventions. Conventions** are the proper rules for spelling, grammar, usage, punctuation, and capitalization. The Your Task section of the writing prompt tells you that you must proofread your composition carefully, when it is done, in order to catch and correct spelling, grammar, usage, punctuation, and capitalization errors. (See page 208 for a brief description of what to check for in your essay.)

ANSWER: There

File   Activity   Edit   Help

> See Movie
> Call Friend
> Listen to CDs
> **Do Activities, Lesson 1.2**
> Go to Concert
> Go Shopping

A. Analyzing Writing Prompts

In this exercise, you will practice analyzing a writing prompt. Two sample writing prompts appear below. You will not complete the assignments in these prompts. Instead, you will read each prompt and answer questions 1 through 5 below about each one. The selections mentioned in these prompts do not appear in this text.

1. What will be the source of the information for this piece of writing?

2. What will be the topic?

3. What form will the piece of writing take?

4. Who will be the audience?

5. What is the purpose of the piece of writing? What specific goals will the writer have to accomplish?

Writing Prompt 1

Text: Excerpt from *Blues People*, by LeRoi Jones

Directions to Students: For this part of the test, you will listen to a reading from a book by LeRoi Jones called *Blues People*, then write a response based on the situation described below. You will also answer some multiple-choice questions about key ideas in the reading.

The Situation: To raise money for your school jazz band, the members of the band have decided to invite several local blues bands to perform at a concert for parents and other community members, to be held in the high-school auditorium. You have been asked by the Music Director of your school to start the evening out by describing to the audience what makes blues different from other kinds of music. To prepare you for writing your introduction to blues music, the Music Director has asked you to listen to an audiotape of a selection from LeRoi Jones's book *Blues People*.

You will hear the selection twice. You may take notes on the sheet provided at any time you wish as you listen to the selection.

VOC: Words with the prefix *mono–*, meaning "one"   Understanding Part 1 of the English Exam   27

Your Task: Write a brief introduction to blues music to be read to the audience on the night of the concert. In your introduction, be sure to

- Welcome the audience, define "blues," and describe the qualities that make the blues different from other kinds of music
- Use accurate, specific information from the selection
- Organize your ideas in a unified and coherent manner
- Follow the conventions of standard written English

(Remember: For this exercise, all you must do is answer questions 1–5 on page 27.)

Writing Prompt 2

Text: Excerpt from television documentary "The Making of *Star Trek*: Remembering Gene Roddenberry"

Directions to Students: For this part of the test, you will listen to the audio portion of part of a public television documentary, then write a response based on the situation described below. You will also answer some multiple-choice questions about key ideas in the reading.

The Situation: Your school literary magazine is publishing a special issue on science fiction. Your English teacher has asked you to contribute an article on the making of the classic hit television series *Star Trek*. You have found in the school library a cassette recording of a public television documentary about the producer/director of the series, Gene Roddenberry. You will use this as your source.

You will hear the selection twice. You may take notes on the sheet provided at any time you wish as you listen to the selection.

Your Task: Write an article on the making of *Star Trek* for the school literary magazine. In your article, be sure to

- Explain when, where, why, and by whom *Star Trek* was made
- Use accurate, specific information from the selection
- Organize your ideas in a logical and coherent manner
- Follow the conventions of standard written English

(Remember: For this exercise, all you must do is answer questions 1–5 on page 27.)

B. Project

Work with other students in a small group to write two prompts for Part 1 of the Comprehensive Examination. Follow the format for prompts shown in this lesson. Base your prompts on speeches or other oral materials that you find in a library.

ANSWER: monorail, monograph, monotone

Lesson 1.3

Taking Notes on a Speech or Lecture

See Movie
Call Friend
Listen to CDs
Read Lesson 1.3
Go to Concert
Go Shopping

Using a Rough Outline Form for Taking Notes

When you take notes on a speech or a lecture, listen for **main ideas**—the important things that the speaker has to say. Also listen for **supporting details**—the comments that the speaker makes to support the main ideas. A **rough outline** is one way to take notes as you listen. For other notetaking forms, see Lesson 1.4, "Using Graphic Organizers for Notetaking."

Rough Outline Form

1. Do not try to write down everything the speaker says. Just take down main ideas and supporting details.
2. Take notes in phrases, not in complete sentences. Begin each phrase with a capital letter.
3. Also capitalize proper nouns, such as the names of people and places.
4. Use abbreviations and symbols such as *Amer.* for *American*, *&* for *and*, and *w/* for *with*.
5. Begin main ideas at the left margin.
6. Write supporting details under the main ideas. Use a dash (—) at the beginning of each supporting detail.

Study the examples on the following page. The trick in taking notes is to put down as little as possible but to record enough information that later, when you look back over your notes, you will find them both *thorough* and *understandable*.

Use whatever abbreviations you wish, but make sure that you will understand them when you look back at your notes. A common mistake that students make is to use abbreviations that they later cannot interpret. Some useful abbreviations and symbols for notetaking are *ex.* for *example,* *def.* for *definition,* Δ for *change,* ∴ for *therefore,* *vs.* for *versus,* # for *number,* and *!* or * to show that an idea is important.

GUM: Every one of the players (is, are) sick today.

Sample Notes in Rough Outline Form

Rick Castro
Wed., April 6

Amer. writers, mid to late 19th cent.

—Ex. poets

  —Edgar Allan Poe

  —Emily Dickinson

  —Walt Whitman

  —Stephen Crane

—Ex. fiction writers

  —Mark Twain

  —Bret Harte

  —Kate Chopin

  —Willa Cather

  —Stephen Crane

Walt Whitman. Photo courtesy of the Library of Congress

Literary movements

—Romanticism

—Transcendentalism (mostly New Eng.)

—Realism (& local color)

—Naturalism

Def. Romanticism

—Started Europe (Wordsworth, Blake, Byron, Keats, Shelley)

—Love of nature vs. love of society

—Individualism vs. conformity

—Liberty (French Revolution, Amer. Rev.)

—Celebrated common people

—Ended in Amer. w/ Civil War, Δ to Realism, Naturalism

ANSWER: is

File   Activity   Edit   Help

See Movie
Call Friend
Listen to CDs
Do Activities, Lesson 1.3
Go to Concert
Go Shopping

 Taking Notes

Read the following article and fill in the blanks on the partial rough outline that follows.

Seeing Double: The Coming Era of Cloning
by Harold Franz

In July of 1996, the first successful birth of a cloned mammal, a sheep named Dolly, took place at the Roslin Institute in Edinburgh, Scotland. In the spring of 1998, Dolly, who was named after the country singer Dolly Parton, gave birth to a lamb named Bonnie, who was conceived the old-fashioned way. A year later, Dolly gave birth to triplets—two male lambs and one female—by the same father as Bonnie.

More recently, in March of 2000, scientists at PPL Therapeutics created genetic quintuplets using a cell taken from an adult pig. Researchers named the world's first litter of cloned piglets Millie, Christa, Alexis, Carrel, and Dotcom.

Prior to the 1990s, cloning—a process that creates one or more genetically identical copies of a creature—had been done only with plants and with such lower animals as frogs. It was believed to be impossible with higher animals, such as mammals. Mammals, such as sheep, pigs, monkeys, and human beings, bear live offspring and produce milk to feed their young. Previous attempts to clone mammals had been completely unsuccessful, but Ian Wilmut of the Roslin Institute succeeded in cloning a sheep. Wilmut took a cell nucleus from the udder of an adult Finn Dorset sheep and inserted it into the egg of a Poll Dorset sheep. He then placed the egg into the womb of a Scottish Blackface sheep. Five months later, the Scottish Blackface gave birth to Dolly, a lamb that was a genetically identical copy of the original Finn Dorset.

Scientists around the world heralded Wilmut's accomplishment as a great step forward in the science of genetics, which studies how traits of animals and plants are passed down from generation to generation. Political reaction to this development was mixed, however. The cloning of Dolly raised fears that scientists might attempt to clone a human being, and indeed at least one scientist has announced his intention to do so. Governments around the world are struggling with the question of whether to regulate cloning and with how to frame any regulation so as not to stifle legitimate scientific progress.

VOC: Words with the prefix *sub–*, meaning "under"

One reason not to jump immediately into the cloning of human beings comes from evidence regarding the aging process in cloned organisms. Dolly the sheep was born healthy and has given birth to healthy lambs. Studies have shown, however, that Dolly's cells appear to be the same age as those of the older sheep from which she was created. The implications for aging in cloned animals could be dramatic. A newborn cloned human infant might start out with the life expectancy of a thirty-five-year-old. Such a frightening prospect militates against cloning humans any time soon.

While fear of cloning human beings raises the prospect of shortened life expectancies or, even worse, of armies of identical super soldiers fighting for some terrorist regime, scientists point to many potential benefits of the new technology. Cloning sheep, pigs, cows, and other mammals could produce herds of identical, high-quality livestock. By combining cloning with another technology known as recombinant DNA, scientists might be able to create copies of animals that would produce organs for transplant, such as hearts and livers. Vital drugs, such as human growth hormone, insulin, and interferon, might also be produced by animals that have been genetically engineered and then cloned.

The transplanting of organs from one species to another is called *xenotransplantation*. Although cloned organs would help to meet the needs of the hundreds of thousands of patients currently waiting for transplants, it is possible that unforeseen consequences could arise with this technique. One complication that may have an impact on the success of this procedure already exists with standard transplantation: the rejection of foreign organs by the immune system. Another potential problem is the transmission to human beings of diseases now found only in other species. Solutions to both problems are currently subjects of study by medical researchers.

Debate continues to rage over possible uses and abuses of cloning, but most of the opposition to cloning is superstitious, misinformed, or uninformed. Genetically identical organisms are nothing new: that's what identical twins are, and clones, like identical twins, are not exact duplicates of one another—they are individuals with their own histories, both before and after birth. While identical twins sometimes give rise to double takes, they are hardly the stuff of science fiction. Neither is cloning. Not anymore.

ANSWER: substandard, submarine, subhuman

Rob McGregor
Wed., April 6

1st cloned mammal & offspring
—Dolly, a sheep
—Cloned in July, 1996 @ _____
—Gave birth to _____ in _____
—Following yr: _____

Next animal cloned
—Pig cloned in _____ @ _____
—Produced _____ cloned piglets

History & process of cloning
—Cloning creates _____
—Previously done only w/ _____
—Sheep cloned by Ian _____
—Took _____ from _____ of
  1 sheep, inserted into _____ of another, placed egg into
  _____ of another

B. Using Proper Notetaking Form

Taking proper notes during the Comprehensive Examination is important for two reasons. First, you will need good notes to provide information for the writing that you are supposed to do during the exam. Second, the instructors who grade your exam will look to make sure that you have taken good notes and may assign lower scores if your notes are incomplete or sloppy.

In a small group in class, study the notes above, which cover the beginning of the newspaper article on the preceding page. Then create rough outline notes for the rest of the article.

GUM: Let me know (weather, whether) you can come.

Lesson 1.4
Using Graphic Organizers for Notetaking

See Movie
Call Friend
Listen to CDs
Read Lesson 1.4
Go to Concert
Go Shopping

In Lesson 1.3, you learned how to take notes in rough outline form. Making a rough outline is an excellent way to record information in a quick and orderly manner. It is not the only way, however. From time to time when taking notes, you may want to break out of the rough outline form and use a graphic organizer to record some information. **Graphic organizers** are charts, tables, diagrams, and drawings that can be used to record and organize information.

Certain types of information lend themselves to the use of graphic organizers. As you listen or read, be alert to cues that indicate that a graphic organizer might be appropriate. Graphic organizers are particularly useful for taking notes on material that is related in a specific way, such as a series of events or a list of pros and cons.

Suppose that you were taking an American Government class. For the most part, you use the rough outline form to take notes on lectures and on the class-related outside reading. In addition, you could use graphic organizers, within these notes, to organize certain information. Study the models in this lesson to learn how you can incorporate graphic organizers into your notes.

Comparison/Contrast Charts

Suppose that your teacher gave a lecture about similarities and differences between democracy in ancient Athens and democracy in twenty-first-century America. Hearing the words *similarities* and *differences* might suggest to you that a **comparison-and-contrast chart** would be an appropriate graphic organizer. Such a chart highlights what two entities have in common and how they differ. You could quickly sketch in your notes a chart called "Democracy in Ancient Athens & 21st Century U. S." with two columns labeled "Similarities" and "Differences." By jotting notes in the appropriate columns, you could see at a glance how ancient Greek democracy and modern American democracy are alike and how they differ. Just as you do in a rough outline, you use abbreviations and symbols in your graphic organizers. Study the model on the next page.

ANSWER: whether

Democracy in Ancient Athens & 21st Cent. U. S.	
Similarities	Differences
—"Rule by the people"	—Athens: citizenship dep. on
—Belief that people should	wealth, property, being male
govern themselves	—U. S.: citizenship not limited
—Representation: citizens	by status, race, gender
elected to run gov't	—Athens: slavery existed;
—Citizens can vote	slaves not citizens
—Belief in freedom w/in limits	—U. S.: no slavery
	—Athens: women had no
	rights
	—U. S.: women have full rights

The Parthenon in Greece

Venn Diagrams

Another way to show comparison and contrast information visually is to create a **Venn diagram.** To make a Venn diagram, draw circles for each of your subjects in such a way that the two circles overlap. Label each circle with the name of one of the subjects. List the similarities between the two subjects in the space where the two circles overlap. List the differences in the space specific to each subject. The model on the next page shows how the information about ancient Greek democracy and modern American democracy might be diagramed.

Venn Diagram

Ancient Athens

—Citizenship dep. on wealth, property, being male
—Slavery existed; slaves not citizens
—Women had no rights

Ancient Athens / 21st Century U.S. (overlap)

—"Rule by the people"
—Belief that people should govern themselves
—Representation: citizens elected to run gov't
—Citizens can vote
—Belief in freedom w/in limits

21st Century U.S.

—Citizenship not limited by status, race, gender
—No slavery
—Women have full rights

Timelines

When you read or take notes during class, it is important to note sequences of events. You may find it useful to create **timelines** to record events. Especially in the study of history, for which chronology and dates are very important, the use of timelines can help you to translate lectures into clear and organized notes. Examine the following example of notes taken during a lecture on the history of the Bill of Rights:

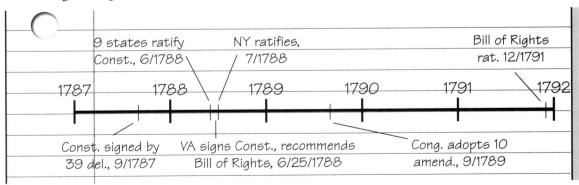

Timeline (1787–1792):
- Const. signed by 39 del., 9/1787
- 9 states ratify Const., 6/1788
- VA signs Const., recommends Bill of Rights, 6/25/1788
- NY ratifies, 7/1788
- Cong. adopts 10 amend., 9/1789
- Bill of Rights rat. 12/1791

ANSWER: laid

Pro-and-Con Charts

Often, in lectures and speeches, people address the advantages and disadvantages of a particular policy, decision, or course of action. One way to organize your notes about advantages and disadvantages is to use a pro-and-con chart. A **pro** is an argument or reason in support of some proposition. A **con** is an argument or reason against it. Suppose that your history teacher is talking about the creation of the Constitution. Many people supported it and others did not. The notes below show how helpful a pro-and-con chart can be in organizing information about opposing positions. Notice that the chart can be embedded within the rough outline.

—Const. written & ratified by Convention	
—Presented to states to ratify	
—Federalists & Antifederalists argue over gov't role, structure, process	
—Pros & cons of Const.	

Pros	Cons
—Gov't can facilitate trade btwn. states —> better econ.	—Too much power to gov't —> tyranny, oppression poss.
—Strong nat'l gov't; good for U.S. in foreign affairs	—Gov't can raise/add taxes
—Gov't can control civil unrest	—Not enough power to states
	—Doesn't address indiv. freedoms

Bill of Rights
—Addressed concerns, individual freedoms
—Limited gov't power

Cause-and-Effect Charts

Discussions about causes and effects occur in almost every class, from history to chemistry. Identifying cause-and-effect relationships will help you to better understand concepts presented in class. Suppose your teacher gave a lecture about what caused the American colonists to revolt against England. Using a cause-and-effect chart, you could organize your notes clearly. Such a chart consists of one or more causes, an arrow, and one or more effects. Study the example on the next page.

                              Causes

        —Unfair legislation imposed on colonists' freedoms
                —Taxation w/o representation
                —Tariffs on popular goods
             —Colonies outgrowing England's rule
            —Colonies gaining more money thr. trade

                                ↓

                              Effect

        Colonists revolt ag. England; form own gov't, Const.

Word Webs, or Cluster Charts

   A graphic organizer that can be used for a wide variety of purposes is the **word web,** or **cluster chart.** A word web is like a visual outline. To create a word web, start by writing the main idea in the center of your paper. Outside this circle write down major ideas related to the main idea. Then, draw circles around the individual ideas and lines between circles containing related ideas.

   Imagine that you are listening to a lecture on the organization of the federal government, and you are using a rough outline form to take notes. If the speaker indicates that she is going to begin to talk about the duties of the three branches of government, you might switch to a word web to record this information. To begin your word web, you would draw a circle in the center of your page and label it "Branches of Government." This is the idea to which everything else is related. Outside the circle, you would identify the branches of government and circle each. Then, you would fill out the web, as shown on the next page.

ANSWER: whom

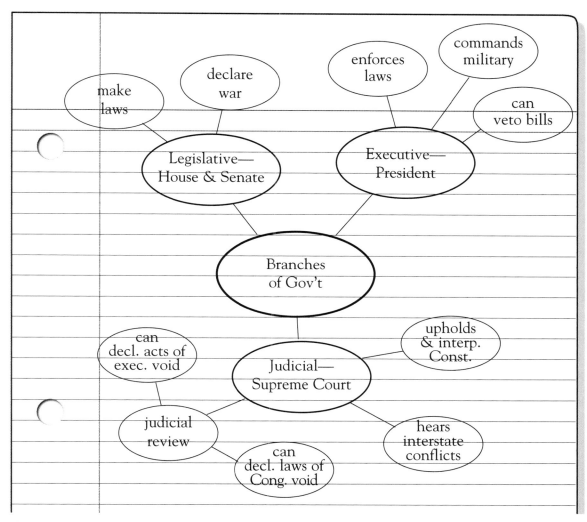

Analysis Charts

A good way to get a thorough understanding of a subject is to analyze it. When you **analyze** something, you break it down into parts and examine how the parts relate to one another and to the whole. To record an analysis while notetaking, you can create an **analysis chart,** which identifies the parts of the subject and lists descriptions of the parts.

Suppose your teacher were to present an analysis of the legislative branch of the U.S. government. You could draw in your notes an analysis chart to record this information. Study the model on the next page.

	Legislative Branch	
Makeup	—2 houses: Senate & House of Rep.	
How formed	—Senate: 2 Sen./state (50 total)	
	House: 1 Rep./Cong. district (435 total)	
Terms	—Senate: 6 yrs.	
	House: 2 yrs.	
Leaders	—Senate: Majority & Minority Leaders	
	House: Speaker of House	
Functions	—Propose amend. to Const.; pass laws;	
	declare war; determine if pres. is unable to	
	continue in office	

Another kind of analysis chart is a **character analysis chart.** If your teacher were to talk about a figure from U.S. history, for example, you might set up a character analysis chart to record important points about the person. Study this model:

	Character Analysis: Ben Franklin	
Man of Science	—Curious, inventive	
	—Recognized as leading scientist of the day	
	—Invented Franklin stove, lightning rod, bifocals	
Man of Letters	—Honorary degrees from Oxford, St. Andrew	
	—Editor of Penn Gazette	
	—Poor Richard's Almanack	
	—Autobiography	
Skillful	—Helped draft Dec. of Ind.	
Negotiator	—Negotiated w/ England before Amer. Rev.	
	—Brought French onto side of colonists	

ANSWER: accept

File　Activity　Edit　Help

See Movie
Call Friend
Listen to CDs
Do Activities, Lesson 1.4
Go to Concert
Go Shopping

A. Taking Notes Using Graphic Organizers

1. Listen to the news on a public radio station, or watch some televised national news. Take notes on the report using a rough outline form. In the course of your notetaking, use a chart to take notes on at least one cause-and-effect relationship described in the news report, such as why employers are having difficulty filling open positions.

2. Read an editorial on the opinion page in your local newspaper or in a national or big city paper. Create a pro-and-con chart in which you present the editorialist's position in one column and any arguments opposing this position that you can think of in the other column.

3. Write the phrase "People I admire" in the middle of a piece of paper. Circle the phrase. Outside the circle, write the names of three people whom you admire. Complete the word web by listing characteristics of these people and by drawing lines and circles as appropriate.

B. Taking Notes on Readings

1. Your teacher will read aloud to you a short passage about careers for art students. The first time your teacher reads to you, listen but do not take notes. The second time, take careful notes on your own paper, following the guidelines on pages 34 to 40 for using graphic organizers to take notes. Write your name and the date on your notes page. Your teacher will collect your notes. In a future class, your teacher will hand back your notes and ask you to use only these notes to complete the following sentences. In order to fill in the blanks correctly, you will have to take thorough notes. Hint: You might use a comparison-and-contrast chart or a Venn diagram to take notes for this reading.

GUM: Alvin is younger (than, then) Alice.

a. The speaker's sister wants advice about _____.

b. Some examples of what graphic designers might design are _____, _____, and _____.

c. One advantage of graphic design as a career field is _____.

d. The tools that graphic designers tend to work with most frequently are _____.

e. Graphic designers should be good at _____.

f. The tools elementary school art teachers use most frequently are _____.

g. The number of students in each class conducted by art teachers is _____.

h. One advantage of a career as an art teacher is _____.

i. Art teachers need to be good at _____.

j. Both art teachers and graphic designers need to keep up in their fields. Art teachers need to keep up with _____, and graphic designers need to keep up with _____.

2. Your teacher will read aloud to you a description of a character from a short story entitled "All the Pretty Little Ponies." The first time your teacher reads this selection to you, listen carefully but do not take notes. The second time that your teacher reads it, take careful notes, following the guidelines on using graphic organizers for notetaking given in this lesson. Write your name and the date on your note page. Your teacher will collect your notes. In a future class, your teacher will hand back your notes and ask you to use only these notes to complete the following sentences. In order to fill in the blanks correctly, you will have to take thorough notes. Hint: You might choose to use a character analysis chart to take notes for this reading.

a. Mr. Akemi is the narrator's _____.

b. You can tell that Mr. Akemi hates to spend money because he _____.

c. You can tell that Mr. Akemi is suspicious because he _____.

d. The narrator is taking _____'s number when Mr. Akemi challenges him.

ANSWER: than

e. Mr. Akemi owns a _____ where the narrator works. One of the things they sell there is _____.

f. Mr. Akemi's eyes are _____ and _____.

g. The narrator thinks that when Mr. Akemi gets upset, he might have _____.

h. You know Mr. Akemi is rude, because he _____.

i. Mr. Akemi says that maybe the narrator is collecting the clerks' numbers because _____.

j. The narrator says that although Mr. Akemi is paranoid, he is also _____.

C. Listening and Writing

Read the following prompt that asks you to write an essay. Then listen carefully as your teacher reads the selection aloud. Take notes *as if* you were going to write the essay. For this exercise, you only need to take notes, not write the essay.

Text: "Walt Disney: A Talent for Turning It Around," by Yvonne Barett

Directions to Students: For this part of the test, you will listen to a presentation about Walt Disney and then write an essay based on the situation described below. You will also answer multiple-choice questions about key ideas in the speech.

The Situation: As part of Career Week in your school, lecturers have been asked to give presentations on various successful Americans. The editor of the student newspaper has asked you to cover a presentation on Walt Disney. You will write an article for the student readers of the newspaper in which you will cover the points made by the presenter in her lecture.

You will hear the presentation twice. You may take notes on the sheet provided at any time you wish during the readings.

Your Task: Write an article for the school newspaper about the qualities that helped Walt Disney to succeed.

In your essay be sure to

- Explain how personal qualities helped Walt Disney to succeed
- Use accurate, specific information from the lecture
- Organize your ideas in a unified and coherent manner
- Follow the conventions of standard written English

Lesson 1.5

Answering Multiple-Choice Questions

See Movie
Call Friend
Listen to CDs
Read Lesson 1.5
Go to Concert
Go Shopping

The Parts of a Multiple-Choice Question

For Parts 1–3 of the Comprehensive Examination in English, you will be asked to answer multiple-choice questions about selections. A multiple-choice question consists of three parts: a **direction line,** which tells you what to do, **a leader line,** and several **answers.** Your job is to pick the best answer from the ones provided. Here are some sample multiple-choice questions: (*The text on which these questions are based does not appear in this text. You do not need to answer these questions.*)

direction line

Directions: Use your notes to answer the following questions about the speech. The questions may help you think about ideas and information to use in your essay.

leader line

1. What was the name of the landmass over which the first Native Americans traveled to get to the Americas?

answers

  (a) the Bering Strait
  (b) Beringia
  (c) Alaska
  (d) Siberia

Multiple-choice formats:

Question 1 is in question-and-answer-format.

2. The archaeological dig at the Dent site showed that ancient Native Americans hunted
  (a) woolly mammoths.
  (b) saber-toothed tigers.
  (c) dinosaurs.
  (d) the pygmy horse known as Eohippus.

Question 2 is in sentence-completion-format.

3. The oldest cave art in the Americas, from the _____ _____ rock shelter in Brazil, dates to at least 10,000 years ago.
  (a) Mesa Verde
  (b) Pueblo Canyon
  (c) Pedra Furada
  (d) Crow Flats

Question 3 is in fill-in-the-blank-format.

Photo courtesy of the Library of Congress

ANSWER: You're

Notice that there are three different common types of multiple-choice question: **question-and-answer, sentence-completion,** and **fill-in-the-blank.** Examples of each of these kinds are given on the preceding page. You may see one or all of these kinds of multiple-choice question on the Comprehensive Examination.

Strategies for Answering Multiple-Choice Questions

When answering the questions on a multiple-choice exam, keep the following tips in mind:

Strategies for Answering Multiple-Choice Questions

1. If you do not immediately know the answer to a question, go on to the other questions and come back later to the one you cannot answer. Answering the other questions might provide a clue to the answer or help to jog your memory.

2. Pay particular attention to negative words in leader lines, such as *not* or *except*. (Example: Which of the following was not a signer of the United States Declaration of Independence?)

3. Also pay attention to any words or phrases that tell how many, such as *all*, *many*, *most*, *some*, *none*, or *a few*. (Example: According to the speaker, all Americans really enjoy . . .)

4. Eliminate obviously wrong answers first. Then, from the answers that remain, choose the one that seems most likely.

5. Remember that on multiple-choice tests, you are supposed to choose the best answer to the question. If one answer is partly right but another is completely right, choose the one that is completely right.

6. If you take thorough notes as you listen to or read the selection, you will be more likely to answer the questions correctly. So, don't be tempted to skimp on taking notes!

7. If the multiple-choice question is a sentence-completion or fill-in-the-blank type, then check your answer by reading the whole sentence, with the answer in it, silently to yourself. (Example: The archaeological dig at the Dent site showed that early Native Americans hunted woolly mammoths.)

VOC: Words with the root *hydro*, meaning "water"

File   Activity   Edit   Help

> See Movie
> Call Friend
> Listen to CDs
> Do Activities, Lesson 1.5
> Go to Concert
> Go Shopping

A. Understanding Types of Multiple-Choice Question

Reread the article on cloning on pages 31 and 32. Based on the article, write six multiple-choice questions. Write two question-and-answer-type questions, two sentence-completion-type questions, and two fill-in-the-blank-type questions.

B. Examining Multiple-Choice Questions

Study the multiple-choice questions given as part of the Pretest on pages 23 and 24. Find one example of each of the following:

1. Find a question that contains the negative word *not*. How does the use of this word affect the answer to the question?

2. Find one example of a question that contains an obviously wrong answer. How does identifying this answer as obviously wrong improve your chances of guessing the correct answer?

3. Find one example of a question that contains the word *most* (a word that tells how many). How would the answer to the question be different if the word *most* were changed to *all*?

4. Find one example of an answer that is partly right. Why is another one of the answers better?

5. Of the questions on the Pretest, which type of multiple-choice question is most common? Find one example, each, of a question-and-answer-type question, a sentence-completion-type question, and a fill-in-the-blank-type question.

ANSWER: hydrant, dehydrated, hydrophobic

Creating a Multiple-Choice Test

Work with other students in a small group to write a multiple-choice test about a story, poem, or play that you have read in class, or write some multiple-choice questions about the selection given below. Exchange tests with another group. Take the test. Then, meet with the other group to discuss the test questions. Explain which questions were well written, which were too easy, which were tricky, and so on. Use what you have learned in this lesson to critique the test created by the other group.

Ahead Of Their Time
by Marie Woolsey

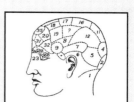

In ancient times, people did not recognize the importance of the brain. The ancient Egyptians, for example, considered the brain superfluous and the heart to be the center of reason and consciousness. Not until the Age of Enlightenment did scientists come to recognize that to a large extent we are our brains.

In the eighteenth century, Franz Josef Gall (1758–1828) and John Casper Spurzheim (1776–1832) made a number of discoveries about how the brain functions. The two scientists then went on to develop an interesting but incorrect theory relating the shape of the skull to personality traits.

As Gall and Spurzheim observed the brain, they developed theories about how the brain communicates. First, they noticed two symmetrical hemispheres, or halves, of the brain. They saw that the two halves were connected by a bridge, called the corpus colossum. They hypothesized that the two sides of the brain communicated across this bridge. Gall and Spurzheim also proposed that the brain is made of cells that connect to the spinal cord and to the muscles. They proposed that this is the system by which the brain controls movements of the body. These theories stand up today.

From there, however, the scientists took a wrong turn. They set out to determine how the brain relates to personality. After many hours observing uneven surfaces on the skull, Gall and Spurzheim developed the pseudoscience of phrenology. In phrenology, bumps and indentations on the skull relate to specific personality traits, such as caution, destructiveness, or generosity. The scientists believed that a bump on the head was due to a brain protrusion under the skull and that these protrusions related to specific traits. In turn, an indentation in the skull reflected a lack of a particular trait. For example, they believed a small bump at the back of the neck reflected an inclination to fall in love easily, while an indentation in the area meant that the individual lacked the ability to love. Gall and Spurzheim eventually constructed a map of the skull with areas marked off for specific personality traits.

Obviously, Gall and Spurzheim's theories about how personality traits arise are not accepted today. Researchers now know that bumps and indentations on the skull merely reflect natural variations in bone structure. However, Gall and Spurzheim's theories on how the brain communicates with the body have been scientifically proven. These eighteenth-century theories laid the foundations for modern neurology.

Lesson 1.6

The Parts of an Informative Essay

See Movie
Call Friend
Listen to CDs
Read Lesson 1.6
Go to Concert
Go Shopping

Writing to Inform

In the Pretest for Part 1 and in the lessons that followed, you saw several writing prompts of the kind used in Part 1 of the Comprehensive Examination. Each of these prompts asks you to listen to a selection, take notes on it, and then do a piece of **informative writing**—writing that provides information. Informative writing is extremely common in everyday life. Examples of informative writing include news stories, how-to books, textbooks, and most research papers and reports. Whenever your writing explains something to an audience, you are doing informative writing.

The Structure of an Informative Essay

An **essay** is a short piece of nonfiction writing that deals with a single subject. The writing prompt for the Pretest asked you to write an **informative essay** on the birth of the Internet. The most common mistake that students make when they are asked to write essays is writing too little. A single paragraph, even if it is fairly long, is not enough for an essay. The safest approach is to create a five-paragraph theme. A **five-paragraph theme** contains the following parts:

Paragraph 1 (Introduction)	This paragraph introduces the essay. In this paragraph, you capture your reader's attention and state the **main idea,** or **thesis,** of your essay.
Paragraphs 2–4 (Body Paragraphs)	Each of these three paragraphs presents a single main idea related to the **thesis statement** presented in the introduction.
Paragraph 5 (Conclusion)	This paragraph concludes the essay, restating the thesis and summarizing the main ideas from paragraphs 2, 3, and 4.

ANSWER: really

Here is an example of the structure of a five-paragraph informative essay. The example contains a complete introduction and conclusion and summaries of the body paragraphs.

header ——————

Chandra Battacherya
Wed., Feb. 6

title ——————

"Looking for Life in the Solar System"

paragraph 1, introduction ——————

Have you ever looked up at the stars at night and wondered if there is life on other planets? If so, you are not alone. People have been wondering since the beginning of time whether human beings are alone in the universe. In our century, scientists have invented great tools for turning the search for extraterrestrial life into a reality. In particular, twentieth-century scientists have used telescopes and space probes to search for

thesis statement ——————

life in other parts of the Solar System. Three places where life might exist elsewhere include Mars, the moon of Jupiter known as Europa, and one of the many asteroids that lie in the asteroid belt between Mars and Jupiter.

[Paragraph 2: Describe the discovery of a rock from Mars containing evidence of bacteria that used to live on Mars. Explain that such bacteria might still be alive on Mars, buried deep in the Martian soil.]

summaries of paragraphs 2, 3, & 4, the body paragraphs of the essay ——————

[Paragraph 3: Explain that a space probe flew by Europa, one of the moons of Jupiter, and observed that this moon has a surface of frozen ice but may contain oceans, beneath the ice, that have life in them.]

[Paragraph 4: Explain that some scientists believe that small organisms such as viruses and bacteria can be frozen and live for a long time. One of the asteroids in the asteroid belt might contain such ancient, frozen extraterrestrial life.]

paragraph 5, conclusion ——————

Will we ever be able to prove the existence of life in one of these places? Scientists at NASA have not yet figured out a way to examine the individual asteroids in the asteroid belt. However, plans are underway for more missions to Mars to look for life on that planet, and other plans are being made for traveling to Europa and drilling beneath the ice to find out whether life exists in Europa's oceans. Eventually, evidence may be found to prove, beyond a shadow of a doubt, that we are not alone in the Solar System.

VOC: Words with suffix –ment, which makes nouns

File Activity Edit Help

    See Movie
    Call Friend
    Listen to CDs
    Do Activities, Lesson 1.6
    Go to Concert
    Go Shopping

A. Outlining a Five-Paragraph Informative Essay

Use the rough outline form that you learned in Lesson 1.3 to write a rough outline of the five-paragraph essay on the preceding page.

B. Planning a Five-Paragraph Informative Essay

In the next few lessons you will learn more about writing the parts of a five-paragraph informative essay: the thesis statement, the introduction, the body, and the conclusion. For now, you should concentrate on learning the form of such an essay. Try creating an outline for such an essay on your own by completing the following steps:

1. Begin by choosing a general topic that you want to write about. (On the Comprehensive Exam, this topic will be given to you.) Choose one of these general topics or one of your own:

   (a) a science, such as astronomy, biology, geology, or medicine

   (b) an aspect of popular culture, such as musical styles, clothing fashions, or modes of entertainment

   (c) an author, literary work, literary style, or movement that you have studied in English class

   (d) one of the fine arts, such as ballet, theater, painting, sculpture, or ceramics

   (e) a person from your life or from history whom you particularly admire

2. After you have chosen your general topic, narrow it. That is, think of a specific topic related to the general one. Examples: the Hubble Telescope, hip hop, the autobiographical writer Maya Angelou, or taking beginning ballet

ANSWER: engagement, merriment, argument

3. Research your topic and take notes on your research materials using the rough outline form.

4. Using your notes, complete the following form to plan the introduction and body paragraphs of your essay:

Paragraph 1: Introduction	**Thesis Statement (Main Idea of Essay):**
	_____
	_____
	_____
Paragraph 2: First Body Paragraph	**Main Idea of First Body Paragraph:**
	_____
	_____
	_____
	_____
Paragraph 3: Second Body Paragraph	**Main Idea of Second Body Paragraph:**
	_____
	_____
	_____
	_____
Paragraph 4: Third Body Paragraph	**Main Idea of Third Body Paragraph:**
	_____
	_____
	_____
	_____
Paragraph 5: Conclusion	**Concluding Statement (Clincher):**
	_____
	_____
	_____

Lesson 1.7
The Thesis Statement and Introduction

See Movie
Call Friend
Listen to CDs
Read Lesson 1.7
Go to Concert
Go Shopping

What Is a Thesis Statement?

As you saw in the preceding lesson, a **thesis statement** is a sentence that expresses the main idea of an essay or composition. The writing topic for Part 1 of the Comprehensive Examination in English will be determined by the writing prompt and by the information you are given. Based on the writing prompt and the information in the reading, you must come up with a thesis statement, or main idea, to put into your introduction. Consider the writing prompt given for the Pretest that begins on page 21. The prompt tells you that you need to write a basic history of the Internet for high-school students who are taking part in a program at a computer museum. An appropriate thesis statement might read as follows:

> Thesis Statement: From its beginnings as a network for connecting researchers working in the area of national defense, the Internet has developed into a popular medium used by millions of ordinary people for communication and entertainment.

Notice that this thesis statement deals with the subject given in the writing prompt and promises a paper that will fulfill the purpose of the assignment, which is to write a guide that provides information about Internet history. When you write your responses for each part of the Comprehensive Examination, it is very important that you include a thesis statement in each introductory paragraph. The thesis statement tells the reader what the rest of the composition will be about.

Writing the Introduction

The introduction to your essay should include your thesis statement. It should also capture the reader's attention in some way. There are many ways to capture a reader's attention in an introduction, as described in the chart on the next page.

ANSWER: is

1. Begin with a startling or interesting fact from your notes.

   By the year 2000, according to one estimate, the number of users of the Internet had reached over 300 million. That is a lot of people, more than the population of the United States, which was about 274 million in January of 2000. From its beginnings as a network for connecting researchers working in the area of national defense, the Internet has developed into a popular medium used by millions of ordinary people for communication and entertainment.

2. Begin by posing a question.

   What is the most popular form of entertainment today? A few years ago, most people would have said that the most popular form of entertainment was television. Today, however, the Internet is challenging television for supremacy in entertainment and in many other areas of life. From its beginnings as a network for connecting researchers working in the area of national defense, the Internet has developed into a popular medium used by millions of ordinary people for communication and entertainment.

3. Begin by quoting someone.

   According to Allyson Stanford, author of *The Complete Student's Guide to the Internet*, "Whatever you are interested in—sports, books, music, movies, clothes, politics, just about anything—can be found, today, on the part of the Internet known as the World Wide Web." Because of the incredible variety that it offers, the Internet has become, in recent years, extremely popular. From its beginnings as a network for connecting researchers. . .

4. Begin with an analogy, or comparison to something else.

   Thousands of years ago, our ancestors invented speech. Much later, they invented writing. A few hundred years ago, printing arrived on the scene. Now, a new medium of communication has emerged that promises to become as important as each of these. That medium is the Internet. From its beginnings as a network for connecting researchers. . .

File   Activity   Edit   Help

> See Movie
> Call Friend
> Listen to CDs
> Do Activities, Lesson 1.7
> Go to Concert
> Go Shopping

A. Writing a Thesis Statement

Study the following writing prompt. Then write a thesis statement that you might use in the composition that the prompt describes.

(For this exercise, you will use only your general knowledge and the writing prompt to write your thesis statement. The text does not appear in this book. Do not do the writing assignment described in the prompt.)

Text: Excerpt from television documentary "The Making of *Star Trek:* Remembering Gene Roddenberry"

Directions to Students: For this part of the test, you will listen to the audio portion of part of a public television documentary, then write a response based on the situation described below. You will also answer some multiple-choice questions about key ideas in the reading.

The Situation: Your school literary magazine is publishing a special issue on science fiction. Your English teacher has asked you to contribute to the magazine an article on the making of the classic hit television series *Star Trek*. You have found in the school library a cassette that is a recording of a public television documentary about the producer/director of the series, Gene Roddenberry, and will use this as your source.

You will hear the selection twice. You may take notes on the sheet provided at any time you wish as you listen to the selection.

Your Task: Write an article on the making of *Star Trek* for the school literary magazine. In your article, be sure to

- Explain when, where, why, and by whom *Star Trek* was made
- Use accurate, specific information from the selection
- Organize your ideas in a unified and coherent manner
- Follow the conventions of standard written English

ANSWER: is

B. Writing Introductions

Imagine that you are going to write the article described in the writing prompt on the preceding page. Choose two of the forms of introduction described on page 53 (beginning with an interesting fact, with a question, with a quotation, or with an analogy) and write two possible introductions for the article using each of these ways of grabbing the attention of your reader. Make sure that both of your introductions include the thesis statement that you wrote for Exercise A.

C. Project

As you have seen, an introduction should accomplish two goals. First, it should capture your reader's attention. Second, it should tell your reader what the rest of the essay or composition will be about. Go to the library and find three nonfiction articles in magazines and make photocopies of their introductions. Bring these articles to class. In a small group, share your articles and discuss the ways in which these professional writers introduced their articles. Based on your group discussion, make a list of ways in which professionals introduce their compositions. Share your list with the rest of the class.

Artist's rendering of the International Space Station. Photo courtesy of the National Aeronautics and Space Administration (NASA).

Fun Fact: The innovative, classic television program *Star Trek* began with a narrated introduction in which the audience was told that the mission of the starship Enterprise was "to boldly go where no man has gone before." The phrase *to boldly go* is an example of a grammatical error known as the split infinitive. In most cases, no word should appear between the infinitive of a verb (go, for example) and the word to, which is known as "the sign of the infinitive." Many would also find fault with the use of the word *man*. Today the correct phrasing might be "to go boldly where no human being has gone before."

GUM: The trees in this forest (is, are) older than me.

See Movie
Call Friend
Listen to CDs
Read Lesson 1.8
Go to Concert
Go Shopping

Lesson 1.8

Writing the Body Paragraphs

Planning the Body of Your Composition

When you take Part 1 of the Comprehensive Examination, your first step will be to take notes on the reading. Next, you will answer some multiple-choice questions. After that, you will do a piece of writing based on the writing prompt. The first thing that you will need to do, after studying the writing prompt, is to write your thesis statement. The next thing to do is to plan the body of your composition. To do this, find in your notes three main ideas related to your thesis statement. These three main ideas will become the topic sentences of your body paragraphs. On your scrap paper, jot down these main ideas as the headings for a rough outline of the body of the composition. Then, go back over your notes and find two or three supporting details related to each of these main ideas. Use these supporting details to fill out the rough outline for the body of your composition. Here is an example of what such a rough outline might look like:

Early Internet as network of defense computers

—Eisenhower creates Advanced Research Projects Agency

—ARPANet links universities doing defense research

—Other defense sites (national labs) connected to ARPANet

Development of Internet into network for everyone

—Early Internet text based

—Tim Berners-Lee invents World Wide Web

—Web, with its links, graphics, sound, and video, attracts millions

ANSWER: are

Internet today

—Includes text, sound, pictures, and movies

—Offers shopping, sports, e-mail, entertainment, research

—Used by over 300 million people

Do not worry about making sure that your outline is perfect. You won't have time, when taking the test, to worry a lot about your outline. Simply make sure that it contains three main ideas related to your thesis statement and some supporting details related to each main idea. **Remember, it is very important that you take good notes, because your main ideas and supporting details will come from the notes that you have taken.**

The next step, of course, will be to develop each of your main ideas into a paragraph.

Writing the Body Paragraphs

Each paragraph in the body of your composition should have a **topic sentence,** a sentence that states the main idea of the paragraph. This topic sentence will come, of course, from your rough outline. The body of the paragraph will present the supporting details from your rough outline. The sentences in the body of the paragraph should be connected by **transitions,** words and phrases that relate the sentences to one another. The supporting details should be presented in a logical order, and the transitions used should reflect that order. Common ways to arrange sentences in the body of a paragraph include **chronological order** (using transitions like *first, second, third, next, afterward,* and *finally*) and **order of importance** (using transitions like *more important, even more important,* and *most important of all*). For more information on transitions that you can use to connect sentences in the body of a composition, see the chart on the next page.

A **transition** is a word or a phrase that relates two parts of a composition (such as two paragraphs or two sentences) to one another. When you write for the Comprehensive Examination, make sure to use transitions to show how your ideas are connected to one another.

1. **Transitions to show chronological order**

   first, second, finally, next, then, afterward, later, before, eventually, in the future

2. **Transitions to show spatial order**

   beside, in the middle, next, to the right, on top, in front, behind, beneath

3. **Transitions to show degree order**

   more, less, most, least, most important, least important, more importantly

4. **Transitions to show comparison and contrast**

   likewise, similarly, in contrast, a different kind, unlike this, another difference

5. **Transitions to show cause-and-effect order**

   one cause, another effect, as a result, consequently, therefore

6. **Transitions for classification**

   another group, the first type, one kind, other sorts, other types, other kinds

7. **Transitions to introduce examples**

   for example, one example, one kind, one type, one sort, for instance

8. **Transitions to introduce a contradiction**

   nonetheless, however, in spite of this, otherwise, instead, on the contrary

9. **Transitions to introduce a conclusion, summary, or generalization**

   in conclusion, therefore, as a result, in summary, in general

ANSWER: coauthor, coworker, cooperate

File   Activity   Edit   Help

> See Movie
> Call Friend
> Listen to CDs
> Do Activities, Lesson 1.8
> Go to Concert
> Go Shopping

A. Developing a Rough Outline from Notes

Go back to some notes that you have taken for another class (a history class or science class, for example). Using these notes, develop a rough outline for a paragraph. Jot down the main idea, from your notes, that will become the topic sentence of the paragraph and several supporting details that will become the body sentences of the paragraph.

B. Writing a Body Paragraph I

Using the rough outline that you developed for Exercise A, write a body paragraph. Make sure to include a topic sentence and several sentences presenting supporting details. Present the sentences in a logical order, and use transitions to show how the ideas in the paragraph are related to one another.

C. Writing a Body Paragraph II

Choose one part of the rough outline for the Internet composition given in this lesson. Write a body paragraph based on that outline. (Feel free to refer to the notes that you took during the Pretest.) Make sure to use transitions to connect your ideas.

Tip for Writing Well: One characteristic of good writing is that it is <u>well organized</u>. Working from a <u>rough outline</u> and using lots of <u>transitions</u> to connect your ideas as you write will help to ensure that you end up with a well-organized piece of writing.

Lesson 1.9
Writing the Conclusion

See Movie
Call Friend
Listen to CDs
Read Lesson 1.9
Go to Concert
Go Shopping

Types of Conclusion

One mistake that students sometimes make when writing essays for examinations is that they fail to conclude their essays. Every good essay should have a solid conclusion. In most cases, the conclusion will be a single paragraph. One way to signal the beginning of a conclusion is to use a transition such as *In conclusion, In summary*, or *As the preceding paragraphs show*. Another way to introduce a conclusion is to restate your thesis as a question. For example, suppose that your thesis statement is this:

From its beginnings as a network for connecting researchers working in the area of national defense, the Internet has developed into a popular medium used by millions of ordinary people for communication and entertainment.

If so, you could begin your conclusion with a question like this:

How did a network for defense contractors become a wildly popular medium for communication among ordinary people? As we have seen, . . .

In most cases, the conclusion to a composition should restate, or briefly summarize in different words, the main idea of the composition and the main supporting ideas. Other possibilities for conclusions include relating the main idea of the composition to the reader, explaining why the topic of the composition is important now or for the future, calling on the reader to take some action, or making a suggestion to the reader for finding more information about the subject. Here is an example of a conclusion that summarizes the main ideas of the composition:

How did a network for defense contractors become a wildly popular medium for communication among ordinary people? As we have seen, the Internet may well have remained the province of defense specialists if not for the work of Tim Berners-Lee,

ANSWER: multilingual, multicolored, multiply

who invented the World Wide Web. The Web transformed the Internet into an easy-to-use, immensely popular means for doing everything from sending a birthday greeting to a distant friend to checking out the latest news. If you are not already on the Internet yourself, give it a try. You may find, as 300 million other people have, that the Internet is the most useful and exciting new communications technology since the telephone.

Here is an example of a conclusion that explains the importance of the topic to the reader:

As the preceding paragraphs show, the Internet has grown from being a private network for defense researchers to being a communications technology with as much popularity and more usefulness than television. Over the coming years, this technology will become even more important, as the number of Internet users grows and as other forms of communication, such as television programs, telephone calls, newspapers, and magazines, start to be delivered over the Internet. Eventually, people probably will not have separate telephones, televisions, stereos, fax machines, and so on in their homes. Instead, almost all outside information will come through the Internet. Getting online today is one way to make sure that you will be ready when that future comes.

 Suggestions for Conclusions

1. Use a transition to signal to the reader that he or she is about to read the conclusion of the composition.

2. Pose a question.

3. Restate your thesis and main ideas in different words.

4. Relate your topic to your reader, showing why it is important to his or her life or will be important in the future.

5. Call on your reader to do something—to take some action.

6. Suggest additional sources of information to which readers can go to find more information about the topic.

GUM: I bought an (Italian, italian) ice in Central Park.

File   Activity   Edit   Help

> See Movie
> Call Friend
> Listen to CDs
> **Do Activities, Lesson 1.9**
> Go to Concert
> Go Shopping

A. Studying Professional Conclusions

Go to the library or get on the Internet. Find three nonfiction articles by professional writers and make photocopies or print copies of them. Bring these articles to class. In a small group, share your articles and discuss the ways in which these professional writers concluded their articles. Based on your group discussion, make a list of ways in which writers conclude their compositions. Share your list with the rest of the class.

B. Understanding Compositions/Writing a Conclusion

What follows are the first four paragraphs of a five-paragraph informative composition. Study these paragraphs and identify the following parts:

1. The thesis statement

2. The method used to capture the reader's attention in the introduction

3. The topic sentence of each body paragraph

4. Two supporting details given in each body paragraph

5. Five transitions used in the composition

After you have identified each of these parts, write a conclusion to the composition on your own paper.

"What's In a Name?"

by R. Pasteur

In Shakespeare's play <u>Romeo and Juliet</u>, the heroine at one point asks the question

"What's in a name?" As Miriam Baxter points out in her lecture "The Origins and

ANSWER: Italian

Meanings of Names," the answer to that question is "In most cases, quite a bit." In fact, most names have meanings that go beyond simply identifying people.

First, there is a large group of names that come from places. The name DuPont, for example, is French for "of the bridge," and might originally have referred to someone who lived near a bridge. Other examples of such names include, of course, Forest, Roads, Woods, and Fields. Among the large group of names that come from places are those that refer to cities, countries, and states. The English last name Gaskins, for example, is a form of Gascony, which is the name of a province of northern France. The middle name of the writer Laura Ingalls Wilder comes from the Medieval word for England, Engle-londe.

Second, many names refer to occupations or professions. Consider, for instance, the most common name in the United States, Smith. This name comes from the English word smithy, meaning "a blacksmith," a person who bends and shapes hot metal using hammers, tongs, vises, and anvils. In the Middle Ages and Renaissance, the word carter meant a person who hauled loads in a wagon. Carter is, of course, the name of a former President of the United States. In Medieval times, the word clerke meant "a member of the clergy, such as a priest," and from this word we get such names as that of Superman's alter ego, Clark Kent. (Kent, by the way, is the name of a county in southeastern England.) Other names that refer to occupations include Miller (a person who grinds grain), Parsons (a parson, or country preacher), Mercer (a trades-man or shopkeeper), Shoemaker, Farmer, and Goldsmith.

Third, many names originally described people's characteristics or relations. A tall person might be called Longfellow. A light-complexioned person might be called Gray or White. A person with a darker complexion might be called Brown or Black or Rosen (meaning "rose-colored," or "red"). In early Medieval times, people often had just one name. They were called John or Jack. Later, when such a person had a son, the son might be called John's son or Jack's son, or simply Johnson or Jackson.

GUM: Marla (asked, aksed) for some more scrap paper.   Writing the Conclusion   63

Lesson 1.10

Taking Part 1 of the Exam: A Summary

File   Activity   Edit   Help

See Movie
Call Friend
Listen to CDs
Read Lesson 1.10
Go to Concert
Go Shopping

The following is a complete list of the steps that you must take during Part 1 of the Comprehensive Examination. Follow these steps when you take the Posttest on pages 66 and 67.

1. Read the writing prompt very carefully. On your scrap paper, make note of the

   • Topic (what you are supposed to write about)

   • Purpose (what you are supposed to accomplish in your writing)

   • Form (the shape that the writing should take—an essay, a letter, etc.)

   • Audience (those for whom you are writing—parents, other students, etc.)

2. As you listen to the reading, keep your topic, purpose, form, and audience in mind. Take down in your notes any information that might relate to any of these.

3. As you listen, take careful notes using a rough outline form. If you wish to do so, include graphic organizers in your notes. Note main ideas and supporting details related to these main ideas. You will hear the reading twice. Take careful notes the first time through. Then, the second time through, take the opportunity to fill in any details that you missed. Remember, taking good notes is extremely important, because these will supply the information that you will use in your composition.

4. After listening to the reading, you will answer some multiple-choice questions about it. As you answer these questions, make use of the strategies for answering multiple-choice questions described on page 45.

ANSWER: asked

5. When you get to the writing portion of Part 1, begin by making a quick rough outline or graphic organizer to plan your composition. The plan should include an introduction with a thesis statement and some way of grabbing the attention of your reader, such as starting with a question or an interesting fact. For each body paragraph, include in your plan a main idea related to the thesis statement and two or three supporting details. Make sure that your thesis statement fulfills the purpose of the writing assignment. Take the information for your outline or graphic organizer from your notes.

6. Write the introduction. Begin by capturing the attention of your audience. Then state your thesis.

7. Write the three body paragraphs of your composition. In each paragraph, state your main idea in a topic sentence. Then write several sentences that present details to support the topic sentence. Use transitions to connect your ideas. Unless you are writing a personal essay or letter, avoid using words like *I* and *we*. In other words, write in the **third person,** not in the **first person.**

8. Finally, write the conclusion. You may wish to begin with a transition such as *In conclusion* or with a question that restates your thesis. In your conclusion, restate in other words the main ideas of your composition. You may also wish to extend your conclusion by explaining the importance or relevance of the topic, by making a call to action, or by suggesting sources for additional information.

9. After you have finished writing your composition, read it over carefully. Proofread it for errors in spelling, grammar, usage, punctuation, and capitalization. Make sure that every sentence begins with a capital letter and ends with proper end punctuation. Make sure that there are no sentence fragments or run-on sentences, that your subjects and verbs agree, that proper nouns and adjectives are capitalized, and that every word is spelled correctly. (See the Proofreading Checklist on page 208 and the list of Commonly Misspelled Words on pages 210–212.)

GUM: The speakers, Jack and (I, me), will stand here.

Lesson 1.11

Posttest: Part 1

See Movie
Call Friend
Listen to CDs
Take Posttest
Go to Concert
Go Shopping

Part 1: Listening and Writing for Information and Understanding

Overview: For this part of the test, you will listen to a lecture about the Reverend Dr. Martin Luther King, Jr., answer some multiple-choice questions about key ideas in the lecture, and then write a response based on the situation described below. You will hear the lecture twice. You may take notes on a separate piece of paper at any time you wish during the readings.

> **The Situation:** Your school will soon be celebrating Black History month. As part of the celebration, students from the school are being asked to write short speeches about great African-American leaders to present in a day-long event to be held in the high-school auditorium. Your history teacher has asked you to listen to an audio-tape of a selection about Martin Luther King, Jr., from the book *They Fought for Freedom.* Based on this selection from the book, you are supposed to write a short speech about the accomplishments of Dr. King to deliver to other high-school students.

Your Task: Write a short speech about the accomplishments of Martin Luther King, Jr.

Guidelines:

Be sure to
- Explain who Martin Luther King, Jr., was and what he accomplished
- Use accurate, specific information from the lecture
- Organize your ideas in a unified and coherent manner
- Follow the conventions of standard written English

Multiple-Choice Questions

Directions: Use your notes to answer the following questions about the lecture. Select the best suggested answer and write its letter on your answer sheet. The questions may help you think about ideas from the lecture that you might want to use in your writing. You may return to these questions any time you wish.

1. **Martin Luther King, Jr., led a boycott against segregated busing in the city of**
   (a) Boston, Massachusetts.
   (b) Montgomery, Alabama.
   (c) Little Rock, Arkansas.
   (d) Los Angeles, California.

2. **Dr. King based his protest technique, known as _____, on the teachings of the Indian political leader Mohandas Gandhi.**
   (a) nonviolent aggression
   (b) direct confrontation
   (c) passive resistance
   (d) civil disobedience

3. **In 1964 Dr. King was awarded the**
   (a) Pulitzer Prize.
   (b) Nobel Prize.
   (c) Bollingen Prize.
   (d) National Freedom Medal.

4. **The 1963 March on Washington culminated in Dr. King's speech**
   (a) "I Have a Dream."
   (b) "The Birth of a New Nation."
   (c) "I've Been to the Mountaintop."
   (d) "Why We Can't Wait."

5. **Dr. King helped to found the Southern _____ Leadership Conference.**
   (a) Islamic
   (b) Christian
   (c) Baptist
   (d) Methodist

6. **The 1964 Civil Rights Act was signed into law by President**
   (a) Eisenhower.
   (b) Kennedy.
   (c) Johnson.
   (d) Nixon.

7. **Dr. King was assassinated while in Memphis to support striking**
   (a) truck drivers.
   (b) sanitation workers.
   (c) transportation workers.
   (d) air traffic controllers.

8. **Dr. King was the subject of a federal investigation because of his opposition to the _____ War.**
   (a) Korean
   (b) Gulf
   (c) Vietnam
   (d) Second World

9. **_____ opposed Dr. King on the issue of nonviolence.**
   (a) Stokely Carmichael
   (b) Robert Kennedy
   (c) Rosa Parks
   (d) Mohandas Gandhi

10. **Martin Luther King, Jr., received his Ph.D. from**
    (a) Boston University.
    (b) Harvard University.
    (c) Morehouse College.
    (d) Emory University.

Lesson 1.12

Proofreading Workshop

See Movie
Call Friend
Listen to CDs
Read Lesson 1.12
Go to Concert
Go Shopping

The following is a list of items you should check when proofreading written work:

1. **Spelling.** Make sure that every word is spelled correctly.

2. **Capitalization.** Make sure that every sentence begins with a capital letter. Also make sure that every proper noun or adjective, including the names of people and places, begins with a capital letter.
   EXAMPLE The young French doctor spent two years in Thailand treating Vietnamese refugees.

3. **End Punctuation.** Make sure that every sentence ends with an appropriate punctuation mark—a period (.), exclamation mark (!), or question mark (?).
   EXAMPLE Could anyone have foreseen the events of the last fifty years?

4. **Quotations.** Make sure that any direct quotations from the listening passage are enclosed in quotation marks ("xxxxx"). Use single quotes to enclose a quote within a quote.
   EXAMPLE Newton wrote, "If I have seen further than others, it is by standing on the shoulders of Giants."
   EXAMPLE Robert F. Kennedy said, "'Give me a place to stand,' said, Archimedes, "and I can move the world.' Those men moved the world, and so can we all."

5. **Verb Agreement.** Locate the subject and main verb of each sentence. Make sure that the main verb in each sentence agrees with its subject.
   EXAMPLE Many types of shark are not aggressive toward human beings. ("types . . . are")

6. **Punctuation.** Check to make sure that other punctuation marks, such as commas and apostrophes, are used correctly.

ANSWER: As

7. **Pronoun Reference.** Make sure that the antecedent of each pronoun (the word to which the pronoun refers) is clear. Also make sure that the pronoun agrees with its antecedent.

   EXAMPLE Each of the Boy Scouts needs to bring his backpack to tonight's meeting. ("Each . . . needs)

8. **Sentence Fragments and Run-ons.** Mark any sentence fragments (groups of words that lack essential parts of a complete sentence) or run-ons (two or more sentences joined incorrectly).

   WRONG The swimmer floating in the Dead Sea.

   RIGHT   The swimmer enjoyed floating in the Dead Sea.

   WRONG The swimmer enjoyed floating in the Dead Sea her body felt so light.

   RIGHT   The swimmer enjoyed floating in the Dead Sea. Her body felt so light.

9. **Dangling and Misplaced Modifiers.** Make sure that phrases, especially those beginning with *–ing* words, are placed correctly and modify the right words.

   WRONG Hanging from the apple tree, Zareena spotted a ripe red apple.

   RIGHT   Zareena spotted a ripe red apple hanging from the apple tree.

   RIGHT   Hanging from the apple tree, Zareena gathered her courage and let go of the branch.

10. **Usage.** Check for errors in usage, such as *I* for *me* or *who* for *whom*.

   WRONG Elijah and me will give flowers to whoever we please.

   RIGHT   Elijah and I will give flowers to whomever we please.

Use these symbols when proofreading written work:

∿ transpose	to boldly go	≡ capitalize	ms. sanchez
∧ insert	best my friend	/ make lower case	John's Book
↗ delete	not hardly finished	— replace	a purfect score
⊙ add period	Ms Chandra	↶ move	a silver beautiful ring
∧ add comma	red blue, and green	⌣ close space	Bat man and Robin
⁀ add colon	Read this	# add space	high school
⌄ add apostrophe	Yolandas jacket	⌶ delete and close	The book is theirs

GUM: Ask (whether, whether or not) Louis has arrived.

See Movie
Call Friend
Listen to CDs
Do Activities, Lesson 1.12
Go to Concert
Go Shopping

 Correcting Errors in Grammar and Punctuation

Correct the errors in spelling, grammar, and usage in the following sentences. Insert correct punctuation where needed.

1. Alan's concience was bothering him after he lead Mrs. Guzman to beleive that he was single-handedly responsable for rescueing her daugter.

2. a russian exchange Student lived in abigail's home in schenectady in april and may of last year.

3. Did Phoebe realize that we were waiting for her at the station

4. The essay entitled What's In A Name? says, "In medieval times, the word <u>clerke</u> meant a member of the clergy, such as a priest,' and from this word we get such names as that of Superman's alter ego, Clark Kent.

5. One of the star players were taken off the field on a stretcher.

6. The childrens' section of the library, has several new titles in it's collection of book's about drawing painting, and sculpture.

7. Every one of the boys are afraid to go into the old barn.

8. The beginning skier. Slid off the chairlift and slipped the straps of her poles over her wrists before she knew what was happening she was flying down the hill.

9. Hanging from his tail, Clarence spotted the little opossum high in the tree.

10. The long hike allowed Daryl and I a chance to clear our heads of daily cares.

B. **Proofreading Written Work**

After you have written the essay assigned in the Posttest on page 66, exchange papers with a classmate and proofread your classmate's essay. Check for all the items listed on pages 68 and 69. Use the standard proofreading symbols shown on page 69.

ANSWER: whether

Part 2

Reading and Writing for Information and Understanding

Increasingly, information is presented to us in images—in charts, graphs, drawings, and photographs. Just looking at images is not enough. Understanding an image involves analysis—looking at the relationships among its parts and between each part and the whole. To update an ancient proverb: Look carefully and you shall find.

Lesson 2.1

Pretest: Part 2

See Movie
Call Friend
Listen to CDs
Take Pretest: Part 2
Go to Concert
Go Shopping

The test booklet for the Comprehensive English Examination looks like the test in this lesson. Take this Pretest as if you were taking the actual exam.

HIGH SCHOOL

COMPREHENSIVE EXAMINATION

IN

ENGLISH

PART 2

This part of the examination tests your ability to read informational material. You are to read an article with accompanying graphics, answer ten multiple-choice questions, and write a response, as directed. On page 207 of this book, you will find a sample answer sheet for the multiple-choice questions. To take the test in this book, you will use your own paper to answer the multiple-choice questions and write your essay.

DO NOT TURN THE PAGE UNTIL THE SIGNAL IS GIVEN.

VOC: Words with the prefix *uni–*, meaning "one"

Part 2: Reading and Writing for Information and Understanding

Directions: Read the magazine article about the variety of life on Earth, answer the multiple-choice questions, and write a response based on the situation described below. You may use scrap paper to take notes as you read and to plan your written response.

> **The Situation:** The United States Congress is considering a bill called the Biodiversity Act, which would strengthen laws protecting endangered species of plants and animals. Your class has elected you to write a statement to be sent to your congresswoman, Representative Shirley Mack, supporting the bill. The statement will be signed by all the students in your school. To help you prepare to write your statement, the student council has asked you to read a magazine article by ecologist Héctor Sánchez.

Your Task: Using relevant information from the article and the accompanying graphic material, write a brief essay, on behalf of the students in your school, supporting legislation to protect endangered plants and animals.

Guidelines:

Be sure to

- Include language supporting the Biodiversity Act
- Explain why protecting species of plants and animals from extinction is in the best interest of human beings
- Use accurate, specific information from the reading and from the accompanying visual materials
- Use a tone and voice appropriate for public discourse on a serious topic
- Organize your ideas in a unified and coherent manner
- Follow the conventions of standard written English

ANSWER: unicycle, universal, united, universe

Our Place on the Planet: Biodiversity and Human Ends
by Dr. Héctor A. Sánchez

Life comes in an amazing variety of forms.

The world teems with life—with billions of creatures, great and small. From viruses far tinier than the point of a pin to giant sequoias over 300 feet tall, life appears in an amazing variety of forms. To date, scientists have identified over 1,400,000 different species of plants, animals, fungi, and microorganisms. The actual number of species, however, is probably far greater. Harvard biologist E. O. Wilson estimates that the total number of different species on the Earth today might run as high as 100 million, or 71.4 times the number known to science. As Wilson points out, one can pick any tree at random in the Brazilian rain forest, shake it, and a number of new species, never before seen by a human being, will fall to the ground. In 1939, fishermen near the Comoro Islands off the coast of Africa pulled up in their nets a coelacanth—a fish previously believed to have been extinct for over 300 million years. A teaspoonful of dirt contains some 30 billion bacteria, most representing species as yet unknown to science. The world is full of a remarkable variety of life forms—insects that live buried in the Antarctic ice, tube worms that live in the absolute darkness at the deepest depths of the ocean, algae that live in boiling hot springs—and most of these creatures—most of those that share this planet with us—are unknown.

We humans tend to think of ourselves as special, but we represent a very small number of the creatures on the planet. Most of the known species of living creatures are insects. Scientists have identified over 750,000 species of insects, including almost 300,000 species of beetles and over 100,000 species of ants and wasps. The next largest group of creatures is the plants. Almost 250,000 separate plant species have been identified, mostly flowering plants known as angiosperms. The higher animals, including human beings, make up only about 20

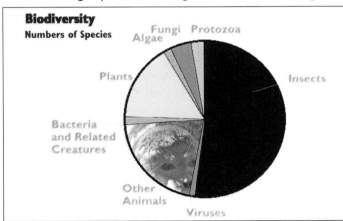

Biodiversity
Numbers of Species

Fungi Protozoa
Algae

Plants

Insects

Bacteria and Related Creatures

Other Animals

Viruses

Known Species

1. Insects: 751,000 (53.15%)
2. Protozoa: 30,800 (2.18%)
3. Fungi: 69,000 (4.88 %)
4. Algae: 26,900 (1.90 %)
5. Plants: 248,400 (17.58 %)
6. Bacteria: 4,800 (.34 %)
7. Viruses: 1,000 (.07 %)
8. Other Animals: 281,000 (19.89 %)

percent of the known species on Earth. Human beings are one species among a possible 100 million on the planet, and yet we act as though the entire Earth belonged to us.

In some sense, it does. Human beings are doubtless the smartest of all creatures. We, alone, have created language, civilization, technology, books, and computers. We have figured out how to live in most places on the globe, from the hottest deserts to the frozen Arctic. We have conquered the land, the sea, and the skies. Our voices and our computer data travel around the globe at the speed of light. Recently, we have taken the first tentative steps away from our birthplace, the Earth, and toward the stars. These are all impressive accomplishments, and we have reason to be proud of our species.

Sea turtles are among the many animals on endangered species lists around the world.

However, it is important for us to understand that with our abilities come responsibilities. We, alone among the millions of species on the planet, have the power to damage the environment beyond repair. In the twentieth century, our technologies have advanced to such a point that they can have dramatic impact on the other creatures with which we share the planet. When, in the 1970s, the World Bank financed a road into the Brazilian rain forest, loggers followed, cutting down hundreds of thousands of square miles of trees—habitats for hundreds of thousands of species that we may never know. In the 1960s and '70s, the waters off the coast of Peru were almost entirely fished out, causing the collapse of an entire ecosystem. The World Wildlife Fund estimates that as much as 92 percent of the wetlands along the coast of California has been filled in or destroyed by humans. All this activity has enormous cost. We are now in a period of mass extinction of species around the globe, and many of these extinctions have come about as a result of human activity.

In the seventeenth century, European settlers on the island of Mauritius, in the Indian Ocean, killed off the large, flightless bird known as the Dodo. On the Hawaiian Islands alone, over 70 species of birds have been hunted to extinction by humans. When the first people arrived in the Americas, tens of thousands of years ago, they found pygmy horses, antelopes, camels, woolly mammoths, saber-toothed tigers, ground sloths, and enormous dire wolves. All were hunted to extinction. In New Zealand, the giant, flightless birds known as moas were also hunted, eaten, and made extinct. When people first came to Australia, over 30,000 years ago, they killed off such interesting native creatures as marsupial lions, Australian rhinos, and a species of giant kangaroo over eight feet tall. In the past 2,000 years, a fifth of the world's bird species have become extinct, and in recent years, the total number of songbirds in North America has dropped by 50 percent. According to the World Wildlife Fund, we are currently losing about 110 species to extinction every day. The Endangered Species Act, passed by the United States Congress in 1974, protects over 1,000 endangered and threatened species.

ANSWER: reliant, observant, compliant, defiant

What is causing these extinctions? The biggest single cause is destruction of habitat. When people fill in wetlands, plow under prairies, or cut down forests, species lose habitats that they depend upon for their livelihoods. It is estimated that 47.1 million acres of rain forest are being cut down every year, putting over 250,000 flowering plants at risk for extinction. The second biggest cause of extinctions is displacement by introduced species. For example, in the 1950s people introduced perch to the Nile River. The perch preyed on native fish, driving many to extinction. Other causes of extinctions include pollution and overharvesting or hunting.

We are in the middle of one of the most massive extinctions in geological history, and most of these extinctions are caused by humans. Still, there are those who ask, "Why should we care?" What does it matter if a few hundred thousand plants and animals, mostly small creatures such as bacteria and fungi, disappear? There are many answers to these questions, many reasons why it is important for people to protect biodiversity. First, other animals and plants provide us with needed medicines. Aspirin, for example, was first extracted from willow leaves, and digitalis, used to treat heart failure, came from the foxglove plant. Paclitaxel, a drug used to treat several kinds of cancer, comes from the Pacific yew tree, and several exotic plants are being studied for treatment of acquired immunodeficiency syndrome (AIDS). Over 150 medicines currently in use are taken from animal sources, including insulin for treatment of diabetes. Forty percent of all medicines are taken from or modeled on naturally occurring substances, yet many species now disappearing have not been tested for their medicinal value.

Second, biodiversity is important to the human food supply. By crossbreeding corn with newly discovered varieties found growing wild in Mexico, agricultural scientists were able to create varieties resistant to a corn blight that destroyed 15 percent of the U.S. corn crop each year. In the 1970s, a virus destroyed much of the rice crop in India and Southeast Asia, threatening millions with famine. The crisis was ended by crossbreeding Asian rice with a newly discovered wild variety. Recombinant DNA techniques promise to make it even easier for scientists to harvest genes from newly discovered species to make better, stronger, more disease-resistant plants and animals for food.

The African elephant is one species currently threatened with extinction due to loss of habitat and hunting by humans. This magnificent creature, one of the most intelligent of all animals, mourns its dead and was recently discovered to communicate, using sounds too low for human ears to hear.

There are other reasons, as well, for protecting the diversity of life on the planet. Many threatened species, such as the Atlantic salmon and the Peruvian sardine, are important economically. In addition, and this is no small reason, other creatures provide humans with recreation and with the pleasure of their company. To a large extent, it is up to us to reverse the current trend toward extinction and so preserve the magnificent variety of life on Earth as a legacy for our children and for generations to come.

Multiple-Choice Questions

Directions: Select the best suggested answer to each question and write its letter on your answer sheet. The questions may help you think about ideas and information that you might want to use in your writing. You may return to these questions any time you wish.

1. **According to E. O. Wilson, the number of different species on the globe may be as high as**
   (a) 1,400,000.
   (b) 5 million.
   (c) 10 million.
   (d) 100 million.

2. **The wide variety of creatures on the Earth is referred to as**
   (a) biomorphism.
   (b) biodiversity.
   (c) biotechnology.
   (d) biotaxis.

3. **Most of the known species on Earth are**
   (a) flowering plants.
   (b) fungi.
   (c) bacteria.
   (d) insects.

4. **Dr. Sánchez cites the breeding of corn and of rice as examples of**
   (a) the importance of biodiversity in providing materials for cross-breeding of domestic and wild plants.
   (b) dangerous, new, genetically engineered foods.
   (c) technology run amok.
   (d) providing new sources of nutrients for endangered species.

5. **_____, a drug used to treat cancer, comes from the Pacific yew tree.**
   (a) Paclitaxel
   (b) Insulin
   (c) Digitalis
   (d) Aspirin

6. **Animals are driven to extinction by**
   (a) loss of habitat.
   (b) displacement by introduced species.
   (c) pollution and overharvesting.
   (d) all of the above.

7. **Animals once native to the Americas that were driven to extinction by human beings include**
   (a) moas and dodos.
   (b) marsupial lions and giant kangaroos.
   (c) camels, woolly mammoths, and saber-toothed tigers.
   (d) sardines and Nile perch.

8. **According to one estimate, as much as _____ percent of California's coastal wetlands has been destroyed.**
   (a) 12
   (b) 37
   (c) 56
   (d) 92

9. **Examples of threatened species that are important economically mentioned by Dr. Sánchez are**
   (a) mammoths and sloths.
   (b) songbirds.
   (c) salmon and sardines.
   (d) moas and dodos.

10. **Dr. Sánchez gives, as examples of human intelligence, the fact that people have**
   (a) adapted to life in many environments, including deserts and the Arctic.
   (b) conquered the land, sea, and skies.
   (c) taken tentative steps toward the stars.
   (d) all of the above.

ANSWER: biology, biodiversity, biotechnology

Lesson 2.2

Understanding Part 2 of the English Exam

See Movie
Call Friend
Listen to CDs
Read Lesson 2.2
Go to Concert
Go Shopping

What You Must Do for Part 2 of the Exam

As you saw when you took the Pretest, in Part 2 of the New Comprehensive Examination in English you must do the following:

1. read an informative selection containing charts, graphs, pictures, or tables

2. take notes as you read and analyze the visual materials

3. answer some multiple-choice questions about the reading

4. create a piece of writing based on the reading

Thinking About the Writing Prompt

In the lessons that follow, you will learn more about reading for facts and opinions, analyzing visual materials, and presenting information in support of an opinion. For now, we shall concentrate on understanding the parts of the writing prompt. Before continuing with this lesson, go back and reread the writing prompt given on page 74. The writing prompt provides a great deal of information about the piece of writing that is to be done, as follows:

- **Source.** The prompt says that the information for your writing will come from your notes on the reading and from your notes on the visual materials. Therefore, it will be important to take thorough notes.

- **Topic.** The prompt tells you that your topic will be the reasons why it is in the best interest of people to protect other species from extinction.

- **Form.** The writing prompt tells you that you will be writing a statement to be sent to Representative Shirley Mack. Notice that the prompt does not tell you, exactly, how many paragraphs you need to write. For each part of the Comprehensive Examination, unless the directions specifically state otherwise, make sure that you write at least five paragraphs.

- **Audience.** The audience for the piece of writing will be a U.S. representative. Of course, your statement will also be read by students at your school, and probably by the student council, before it is sent.

- **Purpose.** The purpose of the essay is to convince Representative Mack to vote for the Biodiversity Act. To do this, you will have to present solid reasons why Representative Mack should vote to protect biodiversity.

- **Organization.** The writing prompt does not tell you, exactly, how to organize your piece of writing. However, since you will be presenting reasons, a good way to organize your writing would be in **order of importance,** from most important to least important or vice versa. The Your Task section of the writing prompt tells you that the composition should be organized in a "unified and coherent manner." A piece of writing is **organized** if the order of ideas in the writing makes sense. A piece of writing is **unified** if its ideas all relate to the thesis or controlling purpose. It is **coherent** if its ideas are connected to one another in ways that show the logical relationships among them. One way to connect ideas is to use transitions. **Transitions** are words and phrases, like *first*, *therefore*, *in addition*, *furthermore*, *later*, and *in conclusion*, that connect ideas. Good transitions for papers organized in order of importance include *importantly*, *even more important*, and *most important.*

- **Tone and Voice. Tone** is the attitude adopted by the writer toward the subject or toward the audience. **Voice** is all those characteristics that make a piece of writing sound unique, as though it has been created by an individual. What tone and voice should you use when addressing a member of Congress? Obviously, the tone should be respectful and formal. The voice should show real interest in and concern for the issue.

- **Conventions. Conventions** are the proper rules for spelling, grammar, usage, punctuation, and capitalization. The Your Task section of the writing prompt tells you that you must proofread your statement carefully, when it is done, in order to catch and correct spelling, grammar, usage, punctuation, and capitalization errors. (See page 208 for a brief description of what to check for in your essay.)

ANSWER: There's

File   Activity   Edit   Help

See Movie
Call Friend
Listen to CDs
Do Activities, Lesson 2.2
Go to Concert
Go Shopping

Analyzing Writing Prompts

In this exercise, you will practice analyzing a writing prompt. Two sample writing prompts appear below. You will not complete the assignments in these prompts. Instead, you will read each prompt and answer questions 1 through 5 below about each one. The selections mentioned in these prompts do not appear in this text.

1. What will be the source of the information for this piece of writing?

2. What will be the topic and purpose?

3. What form will the piece of writing take, and how might you organize it?

4. Who will be the audience?

5. What is the purpose of the piece of writing? What specific goals will the writer have to accomplish?

Writing Prompt 1

Text: "Who Freed the Slaves?" by Barbara J. Fields

Directions to Students: For this part of the test, you will read an essay by Civil War historian Barbara J. Fields and look at some charts and graphs describing the numbers of free and enslaved African Americans in North America from 1850 to 1865. Then you will write a response based on the situation described below. You will also answer some multiple-choice questions about key ideas in the reading.

The Situation: Your social studies teacher has decided to publish a class booklet dealing with the Civil War. The booklet will contain essays by students. You have been asked to contribute an essay called "How Slavery Ended." Your teacher has given you Barbara Fields's essay and some charts and graphs to provide information for your essay.

You may take notes at any time you wish as you read "Who Freed the Slaves?" and study the visual materials.

Your Task: Write an essay entitled "How Slavery Ended" to be included in the class booklet. In your essay be sure to

- Explain the steps by which slavery came to an end in America and who was responsible for the ending of slavery
- Use accurate, specific information from the selection and from the visual materials
- Organize your ideas in a unified and coherent manner
- Follow the conventions of standard written English

Writing Prompt 2

Text: Magazine article, "The Sole of the Long-Distance Runner," by Morton Levy

Directions to Students: For this part of the test, you will read an article from a consumer magazine that compares several varieties of running shoe, then write a response based on the situation described below. You will also answer some multiple-choice questions about key ideas in the article.

The Situation: Your track coach has asked several students to do some research and to make a recommendation about the best variety of running shoe to buy for the track team next fall. Read the article "The Sole of the Long-Distance Runner" and the accompanying charts and write a report for the track coach recommending the best running shoe for the team, based on cost, comfort, and quality of materials. Using information from the article and the charts, defend your choice with reference to the three criteria of cost, comfort, and quality.

Your Task: Write a report for your track coach recommending a running shoe for use by the track team next year. In your report, be sure to

- Recommend one running shoe for the team
- Use the criteria of cost, comfort, and quality of materials as the basis for your recommendation
- Defend your choice in relation to the other choices described in the article
- Use a tone and voice appropriate for a report to the track coach
- Organize your ideas in a logical and coherent manner
- Follow the conventions of standard written English

B. Project

Work with other students in a small group to write two prompts for Part 2 of the Comprehensive Examination. Follow the format for prompts shown in this lesson. Base your prompts on informative nonfiction articles from magazines.

ANSWER: biology, geology, graphology, paleontology

| File | Activity | Edit | Help |

Lesson 2.3
Distinguishing Facts and Opinions

See Movie
Call Friend
Listen to CDs
Read Lesson 2.3
Go to Concert
Go Shopping

Fact or Opinion?

If you look at a newspaper, you will find that it contains many different kinds of writing. News stories present **facts**—statements that are true by definition or that can be proved by observation. Editorials, in contrast, present **opinions**—predictions or statements of value, belief, policy, or obligation that can be supported by facts but not proved. Consider these examples:

FACT: The president's official residence is the White House.

FACT: The White House is located on Pennsylvania Avenue, in Washington, D.C., across the street from Lafayette Park.

OPINION: The Congress and the president should do something to house the homeless people sleeping in the park across from the White House.

The first statement can be proved by definition. The expressions "the president's official residence" and "the White House" mean the same thing, and so the sentence has to be true. The second statement can easily be proved by observation. A person can go to Washington, D.C., take a taxi to the White House, and see if it is indeed located on Pennsylvania Avenue, across the street from Lafayette Park. An easier way to check that this is a fact, of course, would be to look up the White House on a map of Washington, D.C. The third statement does not express a fact. Instead, it expresses someone's opinion about what should be done.

GUM: (You're, Your) not serious, are you?

Proving Facts

As you just learned, a fact is a statement that is true by definition or that can be proved by observation. Sometimes, you can prove a statement of fact by making an observation yourself. Suppose, for example, that the label on a box of cereal says that the box contains 11 ounces of cereal. You could prove the statement

This box contains 11 ounces of cereal.

by getting a large bowl, measuring its weight on a scale, pouring all the cereal into the bowl, weighing the bowl full of cereal, and then subtracting the weight of the bowl from the weight of the bowl plus the cereal. In most cases, however, people do not prove the truth or falsehood of facts by making observations themselves. Instead, they depend on reference works or on knowledgeable experts to confirm or deny the facts. For example, the following is a statement of fact:

Light travels at approximately 186,000 miles per second.

You probably do not have the right kind of equipment to measure the speed of light yourself, but you can look up the speed in a reference work, such as a science book, that contains a record of an observation made by someone else. So, two ways of checking facts are to

- Make observations on your own
- Consult a reference work or a knowledgeable expert

Types of Opinion

There are many types of opinion. The types that you will encounter most frequently are as follows:

JUDGMENTS, OR STATEMENTS OF VALUE: Brussels sprouts taste horrible! Jessye Norman is a great singer. Testing cosmetic products on animals is wrong.

STATEMENTS OF BELIEF: There is probably life on other planets. Even though he held slaves, Thomas Jefferson knew in his heart that slavery was wrong.

STATEMENTS OF POLICY: We should hold a canned food drive to raise money for the field trip. Hector should be elected student council president.

STATEMENTS OF OBLIGATION: You ought to send your grandmother a thank-you card. Ada should clean her room once in a while.

PREDICTIONS: There will doubtless be a colony on Mars by the year 2050.

ANSWER: You're

A **judgment,** or **statement of value,** tells how someone feels about something. A **statement of belief** tells something that a person thinks is true but that the person cannot absolutely prove to be true. A **statement of policy** tells what action someone thinks people should or should not take. A **statement of obligation,** which is really just another kind of statement of policy, tells what someone thinks people ought to think or do. A **prediction** tells what will happen in the future. All such statements are types of **opinion.**

Supporting Opinions

By definition, an opinion is a statement that cannot be proved with absolute certainty. Opinions differ from person to person, and there is even a proverb that says, "Everyone has a right to his or her own opinion." However, all opinions are not created equal. Suppose, for example, that a person holds the opinion that

Studying for tests is a waste of time.

It is not difficult to demonstrate that this is an unwise opinion. All one has to do is to perform an experiment. Try studying hard for one test and see what happens. Then try not studying for another test and see what happens. Obviously, the facts simply don't support this opinion. A **reasonable opinion** is one that is supported by facts. Consider this example:

OPINION: Chandra's older brother is studying to become a pharmacy technician, and I think that's a really wise choice.

This opinion can be supported by facts such as these:

FACT: The American Association of Pharmacy Technicians estimates that the number of jobs for pharmacy technicians will grow to 109,000 by the year 2004.

FACT: Many drugstore chains and many states are now requiring pharmacy technicians to have associate degrees and to be certified, but only 20,000 of the 81,000 pharmacy technicians now working have associate degrees and are certified.

Whenever you encounter a statement of opinion, you should ask yourself, "Is this opinion supported by facts?" If it is supported by facts, then it is a reasonable opinion, one worthy of being adopted by you. If it is not supported by facts, then it is an unreasonable opinion and should not be adopted.

VOC: Nouns with the suffix –*ism*

Often, when people have different opinions, they resort to arguing or shouting or other unproductive ways of dealing with their differences. It makes more sense, however, to look at the relevant facts to see which opinion is better supported. Consider, for example, how courts of law work. The defense attorneys may be of the opinion that their client is innocent and should be freed. The prosecuting attorneys may be of the opinion that the defendant is guilty and should go to jail. Instead of simply shouting opinions at one another, the attorneys go into court and present **evidence**—facts—to support the defendant's innocence or guilt. The jury and the judge weigh the evidence to see which opinion is better supported by the facts.

The following chart summarizes what you have learned about facts and opinions in this lesson.

 ## Understanding Facts and Opinions

1. A fact is a statement that is true by definition (*alma* is the Spanish word for *soul*) or a statement that can be proved to be true by observation (the Empire State Building is taller than the Chrysler Building). If a statement of fact is a definition, you can prove it true or false by looking up the meanings of the words in a dictionary. Other statements of fact can be proved or disproved by direct observation or by relying on direct observations made by others, which can be done by consulting a reference work or a knowledgeable expert.

2. Most statements that are not facts are opinions. An opinion can be a prediction (it will rain tomorrow), a statement of value (most television programs are really stupid), a statement of belief (no ancient Roman could have dreamed up the idea of the airplane), a statement of policy (schools should stay open year round), or a statement of obligation (students shouldn't run in the hallway).

3. An opinion cannot be proved true or false beyond any doubt, but it can be supported or undermined by looking at relevant facts. If the facts support an opinion, then it is reasonable to hold that opinion. If the facts do not support an opinion, then it is unreasonable to hold that opinion.

ANSWER: materialism, Romanticism, capitalism

File   Activity   Edit   Help

See Movie
Call Friend
Listen to CDs
Do Activities, Lesson 2.3
Go to Concert
Go Shopping

A. Distinguishing Fact and Opinion

Number your paper from 1 to 10. On your paper, tell whether each of the following expressions is a statement of fact or a statement of opinion.

1. The world's largest zoo is the San Diego Wild Animal Park.

2. The most fascinating animals in the San Diego Wild Animal Park are the Siberian tigers.

3. Julius Cæsar conquered Gaul, the area that is now France and Germany.

4. Julius Cæsar was a great military leader.

5. The tallest animal in the North American wilds is the moose.

6. Moose are really goofy looking.

7. Great Britain should return the Elgin Marbles to Greece.

8. The Elgin Marbles are sculptures that were taken from Greece by Lord Elgin.

9. The scientists at the Massachusetts Institute of Technology are building a robot named Cog.

10. By the year 2020, Cog should be able to hold a reasonable conversation in English, Spanish, German, or Japanese.

B. Types of Opinion

Number your paper from one to five. On your paper, write five opinions: a judgment, a statement of belief, a statement of policy, a statement of obligation, and a prediction.

GUM: They wanted (to go boldly, to boldly go) forward.

C. Proving and Disproving Facts

Number your paper from one to five. Explain how you might prove or disprove each of the following statements of fact.

1. The average student in my school is five feet, seven inches tall.

2. The Metropolitan Museum houses several bronzes from Benin, Africa.

3. A quatrain is a verse form with four-line stanzas.

4. Europa, one of the moons of Jupiter, is covered with ice.

5. The Korean War ended in 1953.

D. Uncovering Facts and Supporting Opinions

The following materials are pie charts from the Executive Office of the President of the United States describing the 1999 federal budget. Based on the information provided in the graphs, write five statements of fact. Then write two statements of opinion related to this information. For each statement of opinion, write at least one fact from the chart or the graph that supports the opinion.

United States Federal Government Receipts, 1999

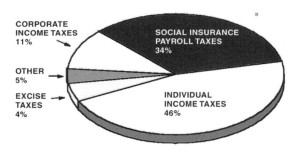

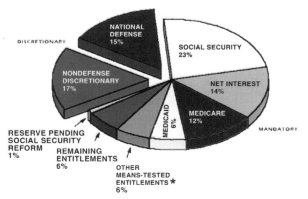

United States Federal Budget, 1999

Source: Executive Office of the
President of the United States

*Means-tested entitlements. Means-tested entitlements are those
for which eligibility is based on income. The Medicaid program is also
a means-tested entitlement.

ANSWER: to go boldly

Lesson 2.4
Organizing Ideas Using Facts and Opinions

See Movie
Call Friend
Listen to CDs
Read Lesson 2.4
Go to Concert
Go Shopping

Persuasive and Informative Writing

Part 2 of the Comprehensive Examination in English will ask you to do a piece of informative or persuasive writing. A piece of **informative writing** presents facts. **Persuasive writing** attempts to convince the reader to adopt a recommendation, take some action, or adopt some point of view. The difference between informative and persuasive writing is that the former presents only facts, whereas the latter presents an opinion and then supports it with facts.

Reread the two writing prompts given in Exercise A on pages 81 and 82. Notice that the first writing prompt is for a piece of informative writing. It asks you to present facts that tell how the end of slavery came about in the United States. The second writing prompt, however, is persuasive. It asks you to recommend one variety of running shoe. To do that, you will have to present an opinion as to which running shoe is best. Then you will have to back up that opinion with evidence—that is, with facts—from the magazine article and from the chart.

Of course, almost all writing is, to some extent, persuasive. The writer must convince the reader that what is being said is credible. Nonetheless, the old distinction between informative and persuasive writing remains useful as a way of examining the relative importance, in a given piece, of facts and opinions.

Organizing Persuasive and Informative Writing

The writing prompts for the Comprehensive Exam will not tell you how long the piece of writing should be. However, you will be safe if you write five paragraphs: a one-paragraph introduction, three body paragraphs, and a one-paragraph conclusion. The introduction should state your **main idea,** also known as your **thesis** or **controlling idea.**

GUM: He (don't, doesn't) have a ticket.

If the piece of writing that you are doing is informative, then the controlling idea will be a general statement of fact:

Thesis Statement/Controlling Idea: The end of slavery in the United States did not occur all at once but rather occurred over a period of years, beginning with measures to limit the spread of slavery before the war, followed by the Emancipation Proclamation during the war, and finally ending, once and for all, with the Thirteenth Amendment to the Constitution.

If the piece of writing that you are doing is persuasive, then the controlling idea will be an opinion:

Thesis Statement/Controlling Idea: Based on a review of the cost, comfort, and quality of materials of the various running shoes on the market, I recommend that track team members purchase Fleet Foot Air Soles for the coming season.

For either kind of essay, each body paragraph that follows the introduction should present one major idea in support of the thesis statement/controlling idea. The major idea of each paragraph should be stated in a topic sentence and can be a fact or an opinion. Every opinion must be based on facts from the reading and/or the visual materials. Here is an example of how a body paragraph in a response to the Pretest prompt on page 74 might be organized:

Topic Sentence (opinion): One reason that it is important to support biodiversity and end extinctions is that endangered plants and animals might prove to have important medical uses.

Supporting idea (fact): More than 150 medicines now in use come from animals.

Supporting idea (fact): Digitalis, used to treat patients who have had heart attacks, comes from the foxglove plant.

Supporting idea (fact): Paclitaxel, used in cancer treatments, is made from the Pacific yew tree.

Supporting idea (fact): Scientists are studying some exotic plants as potential sources for AIDS medications.

ANSWER: doesn't

File	Activity	Edit	Help

See Movie
Call Friend
Listen to CDs
Do Activities, Lesson 2.4
Go to Concert
Go Shopping

A. Informative and Persuasive Writing

Identify each of the following writing assignments as informative or persuasive.

1. Write a letter to the editor of your local newspaper explaining why you think that the state legislature should or should not vote to hold school year-round.

2. Write an essay contrasting marriage in ancient India with marriage in the United States today.

3. Write a report explaining how television has changed over the past forty years, including information on variety and types of programming, number of viewers, and types of service (public, network, cable, independent, community access, and Internet-based).

4. Write a newspaper editorial telling why NASA should or should not attempt to send astronauts on an expedition to Mars.

5. Write a report recommending three novels to be made required reading by high-school juniors at your school.

6. Write an essay that presents a classification system for fantastic creatures, such as unicorns, phoenixes, griffins, chimeras, Frankenstein's monster, the Creature from the Black Lagoon, werewolves, vampires, Yoda and the Force from the *Star Wars* movies, Jack Frost, the Easter Bunny, Santa Claus, ghosts, djinn, the Abominable Snowman, the Loch Ness Monster, Godzilla, mermaids, genies, and HAL (the conscious computer in the movie *2001: A Space Odyssey*).

B. Supporting Opinions I

Choose some product in which you are interested, such as guitars, CD players, inline skates, or computers, and do some research on three different makes or models. Decide on three important criteria for judging the product. Then, create a chart providing facts about the three makes or models with regard to each criterion. Your chart should have this format:

GUM: I (did, done) all that I could do to help you.   Organizing Ideas Using Facts and Opinions   *91*

Product Comparison Chart			
	Criterion 1	Criterion 2	Criterion 3
Product 1:	Fact:	Fact:	Fact:
Product 2:	Fact:	Fact:	Fact:
Product 3:	Fact:	Fact:	Fact:

C. Supporting Opinions 2

Write a five-paragraph consumer report presenting the information from your chart for Exercise B. State your product recommendation in the first paragraph. In each of the three body paragraphs, deal with one criterion, explaining why the product that you chose is better in this respect. End with a concluding paragraph that restates your recommendation and summarizes the reasons for it.

D. Organizing Informative Writing

Write outlines for the pieces of writing described in Exercise A, items 3 and 6. Each outline should have five parts: an introduction, three body paragraphs, and a conclusion. Use the rough outline form described for notetaking in Lesson 1.3 of this book. Discuss and evaluate your outlines with other students in a small group.

ANSWER: did

Lesson 2.5
Analyzing Infographics

See Movie
Call Friend
Listen to CDs
Read Lesson 2.5
Go to Concert
Go Shopping

Visual Materials on Part 2 of the Examination

The reading for Part 2 of the Comprehensive Examination will include visual materials, such as charts, graphs, diagrams, and tables. You will be expected to **analyze** these (to look at their parts and at the relationships of the parts to the whole) and to use the information that they provide in your writing. This lesson will explain how to read and understand common visual materials.

Understanding Line Graphs

A **line graph** contains two parts, an **x-axis,** running across (horizontally), and a **y-axis,** running up and down (vertically). A line graph is used to show how one variable (such as time or cost) changes with respect to another variable (such as number of products or people). The following line graph shows the growth in the percentage of the American food budget spent on meals outside the home.

A line graph

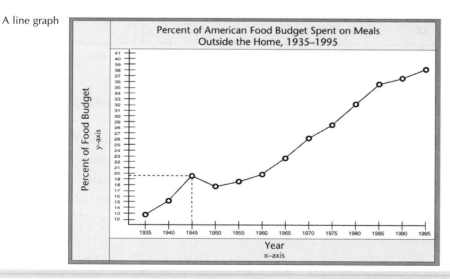

Percent of American Food Budget Spent on Meals Outside the Home, 1935–1995

VOC: Words with the prefix re–, *meaning "again"*

In most cases, a line graph shows the amount or number of something corresponding to a series of variables. In this example, the graph shows the percentage of the American food budget spent on meals outside the home over sixty years. To read a line graph, all you need to do is to trace two straight paths. Trace a vertical path with your finger from the *x*-axis to the line on the graph. Then trace a horizontal path from the point where your finger touches the line on the graph to the *y*-axis. Here is an example:

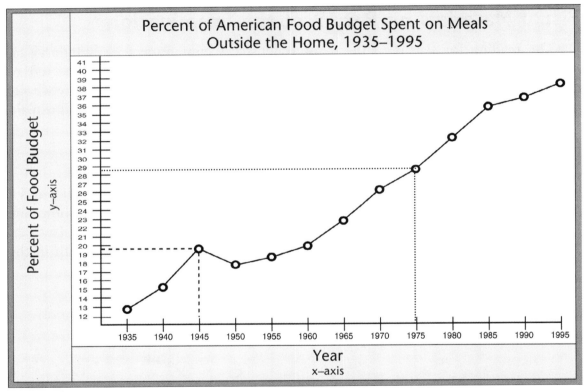

A line graph

The dotted lines show that in 1945, close to 20 percent of people's food budget was spent outside the home. In 1975, it was close to 28 percent. Notice that line graphs are good for showing trends. What trend does this line graph show? What does this graph tell us about changes in people's lifestyles over the course of the last century? To what larger changes in the culture might the change in money spent eating out be related?

ANSWER: restate, reexamine, renegotiate, retry

Understanding Bar Graphs

A **bar graph** also contains an **x-axis** running across (horizontally) and a **y-axis** running up and down (vertically). Bars extend from the y-axis, which shows the independent variable, the year in the case of the graph below. To read a bar graph, trace a path with your finger from the end of the bar to the x-axis, which shows the dependent variable—here, the number of people.

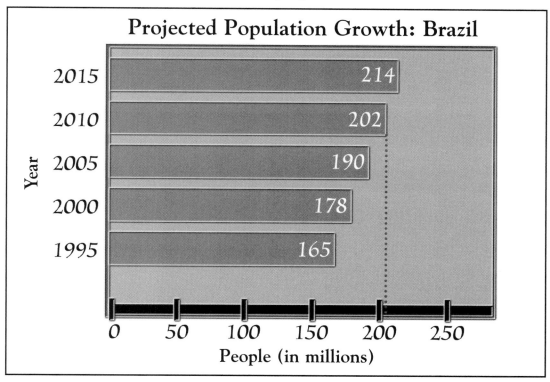

A bar graph

Reading the x-axis at the point where your finger crosses the axis, you can see that the projected, or estimated, population of Brazil in the year 2010 is 202 million people.

Understanding Column Graphs

A **column graph** is similar to a bar graph, except that the independent variables appear on the x-axis, and the horizontal bars are replaced by vertical columns. To read the value of each of the variables, you trace a horizontal path from the end of the column to the y-axis.

VOC: Words with the root *circum*, meaning "around"

Average Monthly Income, by Highest Degree Earned
(for persons 35 to 44 years old)

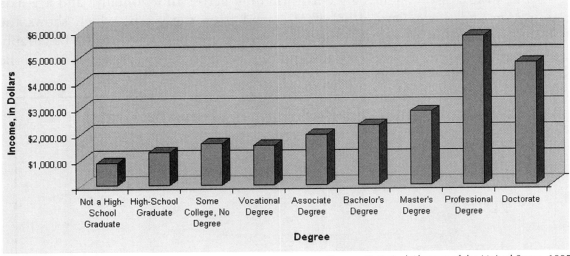

A column graph

Source: Statistical Abstract of the United States, 1995

Understanding Pie Charts

A **pie chart** takes its name from its shape. It is circular and is divided into wedges, like a pie. The wedges represent the "parts of the pie," that is, the relative percentages of the whole taken up by each of a number of variables. Here are some examples of pie charts:

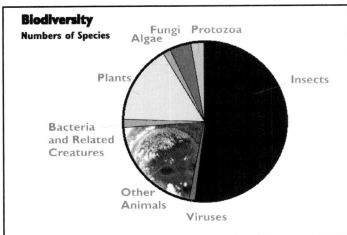

Pie chart showing relative size of species groups.

ANSWER: circumnavigate, circumference

Where the Fresh Water Is

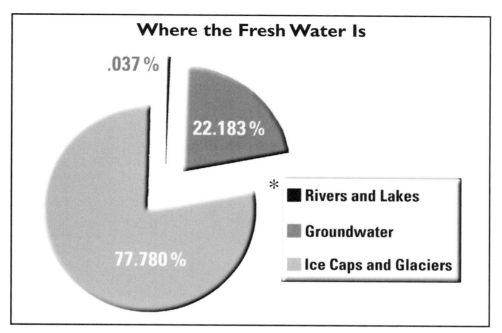

.037 %

22.183 %

77.780 %

*
- **Rivers and Lakes**
- **Groundwater**
- **Ice Caps and Glaciers**

Pie chart showing relative percentages of fresh water on the Earth found in rivers and lakes, in the ground, and in ice caps and glaciers.

*This feature, found on many charts and graphs, is called a **legend** or **key**. It identifies the main variables on the graph.

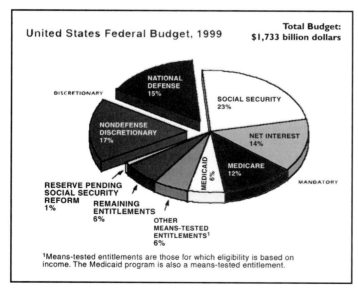

United States Federal Budget, 1999

Total Budget: $1,733 billion dollars

NATIONAL DEFENSE 15%

DISCRETIONARY

NONDEFENSE DISCRETIONARY 17%

SOCIAL SECURITY 23%

NET INTEREST 14%

MEDICAID 6%

MEDICARE 12%

MANDATORY

RESERVE PENDING SOCIAL SECURITY REFORM 1%

REMAINING ENTITLEMENTS 6%

OTHER MEANS-TESTED ENTITLEMENTS[1] 6%

[1]Means-tested entitlements are those for which eligibility is based on income. The Medicaid program is also a means-tested entitlement.

Pie chart showing the parts of the federal budget of the United States.
Source: Executive Office of the President of the United States

In a pie chart, the circle represents the whole of something. In the pie chart above, the circle represents all the fresh water on Earth. In the pie chart to the left, the circle represents the entire federal budget for the United States. In other words, the circles represent 100 percent of fresh water and the budget, respectively.

In both the pie charts on this page, the parts are given as **percentages**, or parts of 100. So, for example, the fresh water found in ice caps and glaciers is 77.8 percent (%) of all the fresh water on earth, or 77.8 parts out of 100. Social Security accounted for 23 percent of the federal budget in 1999, or 23 parts out of 100.

To calculate the amount for national defense spending, you can multiply the amount of the total budget ($1,733,000,000,000) times the percentage for defense spending (.15).

GUM: What can you (infer, imply) from this chart?

The pie charts on the preceding page both gave the amounts of the variables as **percentages,** or parts out of one hundred. Sometimes pie charts give amounts not as percentages but as ordinary numbers, as follows:

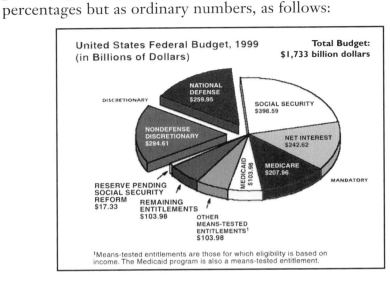

United States Federal Budget, 1999
(in Billions of Dollars)

Total Budget:
$1,733 billion dollars

NATIONAL DEFENSE $259.95

DISCRETIONARY

SOCIAL SECURITY $398.59

NONDEFENSE DISCRETIONARY $294.61

NET INTEREST $242.62

MEDICAID $103.98

MEDICARE $207.96

MANDATORY

RESERVE PENDING SOCIAL SECURITY REFORM $17.33

REMAINING ENTITLEMENTS $103.98

OTHER MEANS-TESTED ENTITLEMENTS[1] $103.98

[1]Means-tested entitlements are those for which eligibility is based on income. The Medicaid program is also a means-tested entitlement.

Pie chart showing the parts of the federal budget of the United States. This chart gives the amounts not as percentages but as ordinary numbers. The title of the chart tells you that the numbers in the chart represent billions of dollars. So, for example, the total spending on national defense is 259.95 x $1 billion, or $259,950,000,000.

Understanding Tables

Another kind of visual material that you may find in readings for Part 2 of the exam is the table. A **table** consists of information arranged in rows and columns, with headings or headers identifying the information. This is an example of a table:

Headings of rows for endangered and threatened species

Heading of column containing information about reptiles

Endangered and Threatened Species

	Birds	Mammals	Plants	Reptiles	Insects	Fish	Other
Endangered	225	303	187	74	11	64	66
Threatened	12	30	62	32	9	33	13
TOTAL	237	333	249	106	20	97	79

SOURCE: U.S. FISH AND WILDLIFE SERVICE, 1991. Note that this chart reflects only those species officially listed by the Fish and Wildlife Service. Actual numbers of endangered and threatened species are higher.

ANSWER: infer

To read a table, simply locate a heading for the variable that is of interest or importance to you and then run your finger down and across, or across and up, as necessary. For example, to find out how many threatened reptiles there are, run your finger across to the column heading *Reptiles* and then down to the row for *Threatened*.

Other Visual Materials: Diagrams, Plots, and Maps

The full range of visual materials that you might encounter on the examination cannot be covered here because there are simply too many kinds of **infographics,** graphics that are used to provide information. However, three other types of visuals that are quite common include diagrams, plots, and maps. A **diagram** is an illustration that shows the parts of something. Usually a diagram is labeled to identify the parts.

International Space Station (ISS)

Photo-voltaic array (Russia)
Photo-voltaic array
Radiation panel for thermal control system
Labels
Service module (Russia)
FGB (base functions module)
Radiation panel for solar batteries
Truss
European Experiment Module
Japanese Experiment Module (JEM)
Node Habitation module

Diagram of the International Space Station (ISS).
Courtesy of the National Aeronautics and Space Administration (NASA)

A diagram, or labeled illustration, shows the parts of something.

GUM: Divide the money (between, among) you three.

A **plot** is an illustration that shows the physical layout of something. Common types of plots include floor plans and architectural blueprints. **Maps** are scale drawings that show the relative sizes and locations of physical features such as oceans, rivers, forests, mountain ranges, islands, and highways, as well as the locations and relative sizes of geopolitical entities such as cities, states, and countries. Maps often contain **legends** or **keys** that show the **scale** of the map (ex.: one inch = 68 miles) and may contain special **icons,** little pictures that indicate features such as cities, recreation areas, or monuments. The map below shows the counties of New York State.

New York Counties

A map

ANSWER: among

The term **chart** is used to describe a wide variety of infographics, including tables, pie charts, and labeled diagrams (such as a sewing pattern or a drawing showing how to assemble bicycle gears).

Whatever kind of infographic you encounter, make sure to follow these instructions when studying it:

 Analyzing an Informational Graphic

1. Read the **title** of the graphic to make sure that you understand what the graphic represents.

2. If the graphic has a **caption** (an explanation, in words, set above, below, or to one side of the graphic), study the caption for further information about what the graphic represents.

3. Locate the **variables** or **headings** on the graphic.

4. If the graphic has a **legend** or **key,** study it to make sure that you can locate the important parts of the graphic.

5. Study the graphic for interesting or important **relationships** among the items listed as headings or included as variables. Look for such relationships as greater than, smaller than, equal to, percentage of, part of, before, after, and so on.

6. If the graphic is a diagram, look for **labels**—words that describe its parts.

7. Follow the instructions given in this lesson for specific types of graphics.

   For **line graphs:** Trace with your finger a path from one variable to the graph line. From the point where your finger crosses the line, trace a straight path to the axis that gives the value for the other variable.

   For **bar graphs** and **column graphs:** Trace with your finger a line from the end of the bar for one variable to the axis that gives the value for the other variable.

   For **pie charts:** Determine whether the amounts shown on the graph for each variable are given in percentages, in ordinary numbers, or simply as pie-shaped wedges indicating relative size. Determine how the wedge for each variable relates to the whole represented by the pie.

   For **tables:** Read the table by tracing with your finger imaginary lines from the headings of the columns and the rows. Values are given at the intersection of these imaginary lines.

File Activity Edit Help

> See Movie
> Call Friend
> Listen to CDs
> **Do Activities, Lesson 2.5**
> Go to Concert
> Go Shopping

 # Taking Notes

Use the information from the charts, graphs, and diagrams in this lesson to answer the following questions.

1. What was the approximate percentage of the American food budget spent on meals outside the home in 1960?

2. By what amount did the percentage of the food budget spent outside the home change from 1960 to 1990?

3. What is the projected population of Brazil in the year 2015?

4. By how much is the population of Brazil expected to grow between the year 2000 and the year 2015?

5. What is the approximate average monthly income of a 35- to 44-year-old high-school graduate? of the average person with a college bachelor's degree?

6. How much greater, on average, is the monthly income of someone with an associate degree than the monthly income of someone who is not a high-school graduate?

7. How much of the Earth's fresh water is found in rivers and lakes? Where can most of the Earth's fresh water be found?

8. Ice caps, glaciers, and groundwater account for what percentage of the Earth's fresh water?

9. Which life form accounts for more than half of the species known to science?

10. Social Security payments accounted for what percentage of the 1999 federal budget? What percentage of the budget was set aside for defense? Which cost American taxpayers more in 1999, Medicare or interest on the debt?

ANSWER: quickly

11. How many endangered and threatened bird species were recognized by the U.S. Fish and Wildlife Service in 1991? how many fish species? how many plant species?

12. What was the total number of endangered and threatened species listed by the U.S. Fish and Wildlife Service in 1991?

13. Is the number of threatened mammal species listed by the U.S. Fish and Wildlife Service less than, more than, or about the same as the number of threatened reptile species?

14. What abbreviation is used to describe the International Space Station?

15. What is the westernmost county in New York State?

B. Creating Infographics

An excellent way to learn about charts and graphs is to create some yourself. Use the information from the table on endangered and threatened species on page 98 to create two graphs. The first should be a bar graph showing the number of endangered animals of various kinds. The second should be a column graph showing the number of threatened animals of various kinds. In your graphs, use a different color for each bar or column and create a legend for each graph showing which animal corresponds to which color.

C. Using Infographics to Support Opinions

Choose one of the following topics and write a paragraph supporting an opinion with information from a chart or graph in this lesson.

1. The Situation: You are president of the United States and wish to decrease the amount of money that the federal government spends. Your Task: Write a paragraph to be read during a radio address to the American people in which you explain which part or parts of the budget you would like to cut. Refer to the information given in the graph on page 97.

2. The Situation: Suppose that your younger brother says to you, "I don't care about high school or about going to vocational school or to college. I just want to have fun." Your Task: Write a short note to your brother explaining why it is in his best interest to stay in school and get a degree. Refer to the information given in the graph on page 96.

D. Taking Notes

Imagine that you are going to write a report comparing and contrasting the quality of life in the poorest and richest countries of the world. While researching your report, you come across the graphs on the following page. Take notes on these graphs, using a comparison-and-contrast chart or Venn diagram. Make sure that your notes include information that shows the contrast between countries with the highest and lowest life expectancies, birth rates, and gross national products per capita. National life expectancy is the length of time that a person in a nation can expect to live, based on statistical probability. The birth rate is the average number of children born per woman in that country, and the gross national product per capita is the value of goods and services produced each year, divided by the number of persons in the nation.

E. Project

Work in a small group to find an example, in popular magazines and newspapers, of the following infographics:

1. Line Graph

2. Bar or Column Graph

3. Pie Chart

4. Table

5. Diagram

6. Map

Find at least one example of each kind. Excellent sources for such graphics include newspapers, like the *New York Times* and *USA Today*, and news magazines, like *U.S. News and World Report*, *Newsweek*, and *Time*. Bring the graphics you find to class and share them with your classmates in a group presentation. In each case, explain how to read the infographic and what important or interesting information can be derived from it. (Note: Do not cut up or destroy newspapers or magazines belonging to libraries or to individuals from whom you have not received permission! If necessary, make photocopies of graphics to bring with you to class.)

ANSWER: ultrasensitive, ultraorganized

Average Life Expectancy

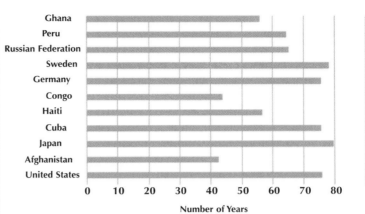

Number of Years

Number of Children Born per Woman

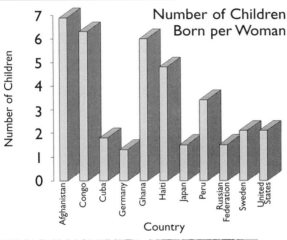

Number of Children

Country

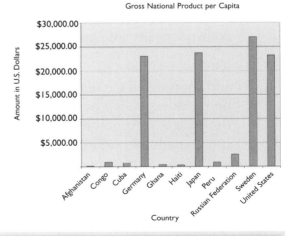

Gross National Product per Capita

Amount in U.S. Dollars

Country

VOC: Words with the prefix *bi–*, meaning "two"

Lesson 2.6

Taking Part 2 of the Exam: A Summary

See Movie
Call Friend
Listen to CDs
Read Lesson 2.6
Go to Concert
Go Shopping

The following is a complete list of the steps that you must take during Part 2 of the Comprehensive Examination. Follow these steps when you take the Posttest on pages 108–111.

1. Read the writing prompt very carefully. On your scrap paper, make note of the

   • Topic (what you are supposed to write about)

   • Purpose (what you are supposed to accomplish in your writing—to inform or to persuade)

   • Form (the shape that the writing should take—e.g., an essay)

   • Audience (those for whom you are writing—parents, other students, etc.)

   • Voice and Tone (the unique style and emotional quality that the piece of writing should have)

2. As you read the selection and study the accompanying visual materials, keep your topic, purpose, form, audience, voice, and tone in mind. Take down in your notes any information that relates to these elements.

3. As you read, take careful notes using a rough outline form. Note main ideas and supporting details related to these main ideas. List major ideas or opinions expressed by the writer as main headings and the facts supporting these ideas or opinions as supporting details. Remember, taking good notes is extremely important because these will supply the information that you will use in your composition.

    ANSWER: binary, bicycle, bifocal, biennial, bilateral

4. After reading the selection, you will answer some multiple-choice questions about it. As you answer these questions, make use of the strategies described on page 45.

5. Begin your writing by making a quick rough outline of your essay. Take the information for your outline from your notes. The outline for your introduction should include a thesis statement, or controlling idea, and some idea about how to grab the attention of your reader. You might, for example, begin with a question or an interesting fact. For each body paragraph, include in your outline a main idea related to the thesis statement and at least two or three supporting details. Make sure that your thesis statement fulfills the purpose of the writing assignment. If your purpose is to inform, the thesis statement will be a general statement of fact. If your purpose is to persuade, your thesis statement will be an opinion that will be supported by the rest of the composition.

6. Write the introduction. Begin by capturing the attention of your audience. Then state your thesis statement.

7. Write the three paragraphs of the body of your composition. In each paragraph, state your main idea in a topic sentence. Then write several sentences that present details that support the topic sentence. Use transitions to connect your ideas. Unless you are writing a personal essay, avoid using *I* and *we*. In other words, write in the **third person,** not in the **first person.**

8. Finally, write the conclusion. You may wish to begin with a transition, such as *In conclusion*, or with a question that restates your thesis. In your conclusion, restate, in other words, the main ideas of your composition. You may also wish to extend your conclusion by explaining the importance or relevance of the topic, by making a call to action, or by suggesting sources for additional information.

9. After you have finished writing your composition, read it over carefully. Proofread it for errors in spelling, grammar, usage, punctuation, and capitalization. See the "Proofreading Checklist" on page 208.

GUM: That movie (effected, affected) me deeply.

Lesson 2.7

Posttest: Part 2

See Movie
Call Friend
Listen to CDs
Take Posttest: Part 2
Go to Concert
Go Shopping

Part 2: Reading and Writing for Information and Understanding

Directions: Read the newspaper article about the differences in wealth among the countries of the world, answer the multiple-choice questions, and write a response based on the situation described below. You may use scrap paper to take notes as you read and to plan your written response.

> **The Situation:** Your Global Studies teacher is planning a "World Cultures Day" celebration that will feature music, food, and fashion from around the world. Each of the parents attending the event will receive a free copy of a magazine, put together by students at your school, containing essays about world cultures. Your teacher has asked you to contribute an essay about the differences in wealth in countries around the globe. The essay should discuss three aspects of quality of life: income, birth rate, and life expectancy.

Your Task: Using relevant information from the article and the accompanying graphic material, write an essay describing the differences in wealth among cultures around the globe.

Guidelines:
Be sure to
- explain that countries around the world differ dramatically in wealth
- describe the differences in income, birth rate, and life expectancy in selected rich and poor countries, using specific examples from the reading and infographics
- use the United States as the basis for comparison with other countries
- use a tone and voice appropriate for an essay to be distributed to parents
- organize your ideas in a unified and coherent manner
- follow the conventions of standard written English

ANSWER: affected

Economic Report Card Shows Continued Inequity

by Elizabeth Brinkman

NEW YORK—The human rights organization Global Watch, Inc., today released its annual "World Economic Report Card," a 158-page report on the state of the world's economy. According to the annual report card, which ranks economies around the world by assigning letter grades corresponding to quality of life, differences among the richest and poorest nations of the Earth continue to be dramatic.

Topping the Global Watch ranking for quality of life, with a grade of A+, was Sweden, with a gross national product (GNP) of $27,010 per person and an average life expectancy at birth of 78.3 years. Gross national product is a measure of the total amount of goods and services produced in a country in a year's time. The per person, or per capita, GNP is determined by dividing this total annual value by the number of persons in the nation. At the bottom of the list was Afghanistan, with a GNP per person of $175 and an average life expectancy of only 42.5 years.

The United States continued to do extremely well in the Global Watch rankings, placing third among the world's countries with a grade of A, a per capita GNP of $23,240, an average life expectancy of 75.9 years, and an average birth rate, per female citizen, of 2.1 children. However, the United States lagged behind both Sweden and Japan in life expectancy and GNP per capita.

For the third straight year, Japan led the list in life expectancy. A Japanese child born today can expect to live 79.5 years, the report said.

Also for the third straight year, income and life expectancy fell in the Russian Federation. The economic woes of the former member of the Soviet bloc are underscored by its extremely low GNP of $2,510 per person, less than one tenth of the per capita GNP of Sweden. "What this means," said Global Watch director Myron Fieldman, "is that the Russian Federation is producing only $2,510 worth of goods and services per person in a year's time, as opposed to $23,240 worth in the United States. Obviously, the average Russian citizen is far worse off than the average American."

The low Russian per capita GNP could be a source of political instability. "If people in Russia continue to be hungry and unemployed, and if the developed countries don't do something, then I worry that Russia might be ripe for takeover by Communists or by Fascists. It really could happen," Mr. Fieldman said.

Most troubling in the new Economic Report Card, however, is the continued dramatic difference between among the wealthiest and poorest nations of the Earth. Twenty-eight percent of the people of the world control 80 percent of the wealth. Among the wealthiest nations are industrial states, such as Sweden, Japan, the United States, and Germany, and oil-rich states, such

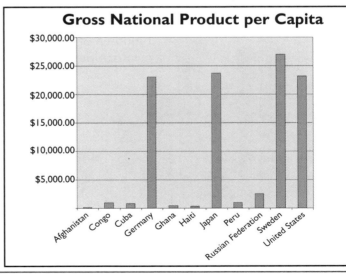

Gross National Product per Capita

as Kuwait and Saudi Arabia. Among the poorest are such African countries as Congo, Chad, Ethiopia, and Ghana; such Caribbean and Latin American countries as Peru, Ecuador, Cuba, and Haiti; such Asian countries as Java and New Guinea; and such former members of the Soviet bloc as Afghanistan, Albania, Romania, and Bulgaria.

According to the report, 1.5 billion of the world's people, roughly a fifth of the global population, live in extreme poverty, on less than $370 per person per year. Worldwide, fifty children are born into poverty every minute. Nearly 800 million people, 20 percent of the population of the developing world, suffer from hunger or malnutrition. Most of these people—62 percent of the hungry people of the world—live in Asia.

On a positive note, the overall life expectancy in the developing countries has risen, since 1960,

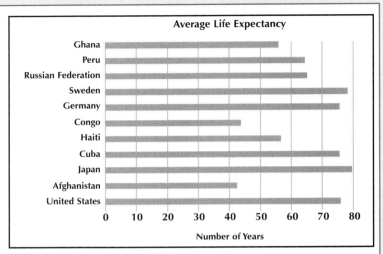

by more than a third, from 46 to 62 years. In many parts of the world, however, life expectancy continues to be quite low. Average life expectancy in Congo, for example, is only 44 years and in Ghana, only 56.

Birth rates are also declining, on average. The total birth rate for women in developing countries dropped from 5.7 children per woman in 1970 to about 3.5 per

woman this year. However, in some places, rates continue to be high. The average woman in Afghanistan gives birth to an astonishing 6.9 children in her lifetime. In Congo, the number is 6.3. In Ghana, it is 6.0. In contrast, women in developed countries continue to give birth to fewer children. Average birth rates per woman in Japan and Germany, for example, are 1.5 and 1.3, respectively, while the U. S. has an average birth rate per woman of 2.1, slightly above the rate of zero population growth (ZPG). Overall, the world's population is expected to swell to over 10 billion in the next thirty years.

Among other positive notes in the report is an overall increase in democracy worldwide. Two-thirds of the people of the world now live in countries with democratic or representative governments. In addition, global crime rates have decreased, and access to health services has increased.

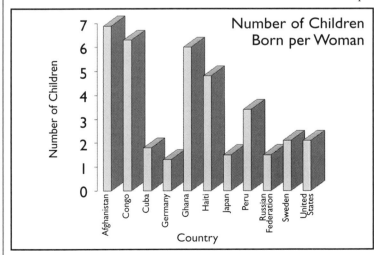

ANSWER: as

Multiple-Choice Questions

Directions: Select the best suggested answer to each question and write its letter on your answer sheet. The questions may help you think of ideas and information to use in your writing. You may return to these questions any time you wish.

1. According to the Global Watch Economic Report Card, the country with the highest overall quality of life is
   (a) the United States.
   (b) Germany.
   (c) Japan.
   (d) Sweden.

2. According to the article, the differences in quality of life between the richest and poorest countries are
   (a) increasing.
   (b) dramatic.
   (c) less than they were.
   (d) nonexistent.

3. According to the article, 28 percent of the world's people control _____ percent of the world's wealth.
   (a) 20
   (b) 50
   (c) 80
   (d) 100

4. On average, the number of children born to each woman in Afghanistan is
   (a) 1.5.
   (b) 2.1.
   (c) 5.4.
   (d) 6.9.

5. The difference between the Gross National Product per person in the United States and Afghanistan is $_____ per year.
   (a) 450
   (b) 2,510
   (c) 23.065
   (d) 27,010

6. According to the report, 20 percent of the _____ suffer from malnutrition.
   (a) people of the developed countries
   (b) people of the developing countries
   (c) world's population
   (d) U.S. population

7. According to the article, overall life expectancy in developing countries has
   (a) stayed the same.
   (b) dropped.
   (c) risen.
   (d) dropped dramatically.

8. The wealthiest countries of the world are the
   (a) industrialized nations and nations with a lot of oil.
   (b) former members of the Soviet bloc.
   (c) Latin American countries, such as Peru and Ecuador.
   (d) countries with the highest birth rates.

9. _____ of the global population lives in extreme poverty.
   (a) One tenth
   (b) One fifth
   (c) One third
   (d) Half

10. According to the article, 62 percent of the world's hungry people live in
    (a) Afghanistan.
    (b) the Middle East.
    (c) Africa.
    (d) Asia.

Lesson 2.8
Proofreading Workshop

See Movie
Call Friend
Listen to CDs
Do Activity, Lesson 2.8
Go to Concert
Go Shopping

After you have written the essay assigned in the Posttest on page 108, exchange papers with a classmate and proofread your classmate's essay. Use the proofreading symbols shown in the table below to mark corrections. Check to make sure that:

1. every word is spelled correctly

2. names and sentences start with capital letters

3. all sentences have end marks

4. quotation marks are used correctly

5. verbs and subjects agree

6. pronouns and antecedents agree

7. punctuation marks are used correctly

8. there are no sentence fragments or run-ons

9. there are no dangling or misplaced modifiers

10. usage is standard

⌒ transpose	to boldly go	≡ capitalize	ms. sanchez
∧ insert	best / my friend	/ make lower case	John's Book
⟋ delete	not hardly finished	— replace	a purfect score (e)
⊙ add period	Ms Chandra	⌒ move	a silver (beautiful) ring
⋏ add comma	red blue, and green	⌣ close space	Bat man and Robin
⁀ add colon	Read this	# add space	highschool
⌄ add apostrophe	Yolandas jacket	⊥ delete and close	The book is theirs

ANSWER: have

Part 3

Reading and Writing
for Literary Response

As Hamlet tells the players, literature is a mirror held up to nature, but literature is a <u>magic mirror</u>. It shows us not only the surface appearances but also the innermost thoughts and feelings. Reading a poem, story, or play gives us a unique opportunity to see inside other people, to share their subjective experiences, to learn how they are both very similar to and very different from ourselves.

Lesson 3.1
Pretest: Part 3

See Movie
Call Friend
Listen to CDs
Read Lesson 3.1
Go to Concert
Go Shopping

The test booklet for the Comprehensive English Examination will look similar to what you find in this lesson. Take this Pretest as if you were taking the actual exam.

HIGH SCHOOL

COMPREHENSIVE EXAMINATION

IN

ENGLISH

PART 3

This part of the examination tests your ability to understand literary selections. You are to read two selections, answer ten multiple-choice questions, and write a response, as directed. On page 207 of this book, you will find a sample answer sheet for the multiple-choice questions. To take the test in this book, you will use your own paper to answer the multiple-choice questions and write your essay.

DO NOT TURN THE PAGE UNTIL THE SIGNAL IS GIVEN.

Part 3: Reading and Writing for Literary Response

Directions: Read the poem "Death, Be Not Proud" on page 117 and the selection from "The Death of Iván Illych" on pages 118 and 119. Write the letter of the answer to each multiple-choice question on your answer sheet. Then write the essay as described in Your Task. You may use scrap paper to take notes as you read and to plan your written response.

Your Task:

> After you have read the passages and answered the multiple-choice questions, write a unified essay contrasting the attitudes toward death held by the speaker of the poem and the character in the short story. In your essay, use ideas from both passages to develop your thesis. Using evidence from each passage, show how specific literary elements and techniques are used to convey the attitudes expressed in the selections.

Guidelines:

Be sure to

- Discuss the conflicting attitudes toward death revealed in the selections

- Show how specific literary elements (e.g., theme, irony, and characterization) and specific techniques (e.g., personification, metaphor, and parallelism) help to convey the attitudes expressed in each selection

- Organize your ideas in a unified and coherent manner

- Follow the conventions of standard written English

Important Tip: Pay close attention to the multiple-choice questions. These will give you hints about important ideas that you might want to use in your essay.

ANSWER: should've

Death, Be Not Proud

by John Donne

Death, be not proud, though some have callèd thee
Mighty and dreadful, for thou art not so;
For those whom thou think'st thou dost overthrow
Die not, poor Death, nor yet canst thou kill me.
From rest and sleep, which but thy pictures be,
Much pleasure; then from thee much more must flow,
And soonest our best men with thee do go,
Rest of their bones, and soul's delivery.
Thou art slave to fate, chance, kings, and desperate men,
And dost with poison, war, and sickness dwell,
And poppy or charms can make us sleep as well
And better than thy stroke; why swell'st thou then?
One short sleep past, we wake eternally
And death shall be no more; Death, thou shalt die.

GUM: (We and they, Them and us) are going.

from "The Death of Iván Illych"

by Leo Tolstoy, translated by Robin Lamb

Iván Illych recognized that his death was approaching, and he felt nothing but despair, day and night.

In the deepest part of himself, in his heart's core, he knew that he was dying. He refused, however, to give admittance to the thought. He would not—could not, in fact—entertain such a simple but somehow absurd concept. Death, that unwelcome guest, was simply unacceptable in the parlor of his consciousness.

In his school days he had read in Kiesewetter's *Outline of Logic* this straightforward argument:

Caius is a man.
All men are mortal.
Therefore, Caius is mortal.

The argument certainly made sense when applied to Caius, but Iván Illych could not believe it true, as well, of himself. Caius was an abstraction, and people in the abstract were, of course, mortal. Death came to them all, no doubt about it. It was a matter of logic, as any schoolboy could tell you. But Iván Illych was not some logical abstraction. He was flesh-and-blood. He was unique, different. He had been a child, delighting in his toys. He had been called Vanya. He had had a mamma and a papa and a nurse. He had had joys and delights, griefs and sorrows. It was no abstract Vanya who had played with a ball, kissed his mother, complained about the food at school. It was no abstract young man who had fallen in love, who had risen to become a respectable man, a public prosecutor. Abstract men like Caius could die, but surely not Iván Illych, that universe of thoughts and emotions and experiences. How could all those thoughts and emotions and experiences, all that he was, all that he had been or would be, simply disappear? Impossible! It could not be the case. The very thought filled Iván Illych with horror and disgust.

ANSWER: We and they

"Surely," he said to himself, "If I were going to die, I would have known about it. I would have felt death creeping upon me like a highwayman or a thief in a dark alleyway. I am told that I am going to die, but this cannot be so! It makes no sense. No sense at all."

Iván Illych tried not to think of it, but the effort, and his illness, tired him. It was like trying not to think of a toothache when one has, in fact, a toothache. As soon as he slammed the door in the face of the unwelcome guest, he heard again the ghastly knocking at the door of his consciousness, as if some terrible person, a bill collector—or worse, a murderer—were outside and demanding entrance.

GUM: The milk tasted (bad, badly).

Multiple-Choice Questions

Directions: Select the best suggested answer and write its letter on your answer sheet. The questions may help you think about ideas and information from the selections that you might want to use in your writing. You may return to these questions any time you wish.

1. **In John Donne's "Death, Be Not Proud," the speaker addresses death in a tone that can best be described as**
   (a) grateful.
   (b) sarcastic and dismissive.
   (c) fearful.
   (d) amused.

2. **The title character in the selection from "The Death of Iván Illych" refuses to accept that he**
   (a) has a boring job and life.
   (b) is no longer young.
   (c) will die like other men.
   (d) is flesh and blood.

3. **The reference to "death creeping upon me like a highwayman or a thief in a dark alleyway" is an example of**
   (a) alliteration.
   (b) personification.
   (c) a surprise ending.
   (d) understatement.

4. **In Donne's poem, death is described as a slave to**
   (a) fate.
   (b) kings.
   (c) desperate men.
   (d) all of the above.

5. **One irony in Donne's poem is that the dead are said to**
   (a) sleep.
   (b) be pictures.
   (c) wake eternally.
   (d) be prideful.

6. **Which statement best expresses the poet's attitude toward death?**
   (a) Death is "mighty and dreadful."
   (b) Death can conquer him.
   (c) Death will bring even more pleasure than rest and sleep do.
   (d) Death is to be feared.

ANSWER: bad

7. **Tolstoy's description of consciousness as a parlor and death as an unwelcome guest is an example of**
   - (a) personification.
   - (b) extended metaphor.
   - (c) simile.
   - (d) tone.

8. **The emotions felt by Iván Illych can best be described as**
   - (a) humility and resignation.
   - (b) anger and anxiousness.
   - (c) hope and expectation.
   - (d) despair and denial.

9. **Thinking about the argument from Kiesewetter's *Outline of Logic* leads Iván Illych to review**
   - (a) other logic texts.
   - (b) his hopes for the future.
   - (c) the major events in his life.
   - (d) the list of friends who have passed away.

10. **Which statement best describes the respective attitudes of Illych and the poem's speaker toward death?**
    - (a) Illych scorns death and the speaker welcomes it.
    - (b) Illych fears death and the speaker scorns death.
    - (c) Illych is indifferent and the speaker is ironic.
    - (d) Both take comfort in the idea of an afterlife.

GUM: The spring air smells (sweet, sweetly).

Lesson 3.2

Understanding Part 3 of the English Exam

File   Activity   Edit   Help

See Movie
Call Friend
Listen to CDs
Read Lesson 3.2
Go to Concert
Go Shopping

What You Must Do for Part 3 of the Exam

As you saw when you took the Pretest, in Part 3 of the New Comprehensive Examination in English you must do the following:

1. Read two literary selections

2. Take notes as you read

3. Answer some multiple-choice questions about the selections

4. Write an essay that compares the two selections with respect to some feature and that refers to literary elements and techniques used in the selections

Thinking About the Writing Prompt

In the lessons that follow, you will review common literary elements and techniques and learn some procedures for interpreting different kinds of literary work. For now, we will concentrate on understanding the parts of the writing prompt. Before continuing with this lesson, go back and reread the writing prompt given on page 116. The writing prompt provides a great deal of information about the essay that you must write, as follows:

- **Source.** The prompt tells you that you will be writing about two literary selections, a poem and an excerpt from a short story. You will want to take notes on information in these works that is related to the topic of the essay.

- **Topic.** The prompt says that the topic is a comparison of the attitudes toward death found in the two selections, with a focus on how they differ.

- **Form.** Your writing should be in the form of an essay, which is a short composition that expresses your understanding of a subject. Unless the directions tell you otherwise, write at least five solid paragraphs.

ANSWER: sweet

- **Purpose.** The purpose of the essay is to contrast the attitudes toward death held by the speaker of the poem and the character in the short story. In your writing, you must explain how specific literary elements and techniques are used to convey these attitudes.

- **Organization.** The writing prompt does not give specific instructions regarding the organization of your essay, but a five-paragraph structure would provide a good organizational scheme. Your introductory paragraph could capture the attention of your reader, name the titles and authors of the two works, and state the thesis that you will be setting forth. Each of the body paragraphs could contain a topic sentence that presents one way in which the two attitudes toward death differ and evidence from the works to support the topic sentence. The concluding paragraph could wrap up your arguments in a summary statement.

  The guidelines in the prompt tell you to "organize your ideas in a unified and coherent manner." A piece of writing is **organized** if the order of its ideas makes sense. A piece of writing is **unified** if its ideas all relate to its thesis or controlling purpose. It is **coherent** if its ideas are connected to one another in ways that show the logical relationships among them. One way to connect ideas is to use transitions, such as *first, therefore, furthermore, on the other hand, similarly, more importantly,* and *in conclusion,* that connect one idea or group of ideas to the next.

- **Development.** The prompt instructs you to show how specific literary elements and techniques convey the attitudes expressed in each selection. To fulfill this portion of the task, you will need to refer to particular elements and techniques used in the selections. For more information, see Lesson 3.3, "Literary Genres, Elements, and Techniques." For help in interpreting a poem, see Lesson 3.4, "Reading a Lyric Poem." For guidelines for understanding a story, see Lesson 3.5, "Reading a Narrative."

  When you present evidence from the works, you will paraphrase, summarize, or quote from them. It is best to use a combination of the three. For information about how to incorporate specific references to literary works into your writing, see Lesson 3.6, "Using Quotations as Evidence in Your Writing."

- **Conventions.** The Your Task section of the writing prompt tells you to follow the conventions of standard written English. **Conventions** are the proper rules for spelling, grammar, punctuation, and capitalization.

GUM: Marco (did, done) most of the work.

File	Activity	Edit	Help

See Movie
Call Friend
Listen to CDs
Do Activities, Lesson 3.2
Go to Concert
Go Shopping

A. Analyzing Writing Prompts

In this exercise, you will practice analyzing a writing prompt. Two sample writing prompts appear below. You will not complete the assignments in these prompts. Instead, you will read each prompt and answer questions 1 through 4 below about each one. The selections mentioned in these prompts do not appear in this text.

1. What will be the sources of the information for this piece of writing?

2. What will be the topic?

3. What form will the piece of writing take, and how might you organize it?

4. What is the purpose of the piece of writing? What specific goals will the writer have to accomplish?

Writing Prompt 1

Texts: Excerpt from the short story "Araby," by James Joyce, and the poem "A Dream Deferred," by Langston Hughes

Directions to Students: For this part of the test, you will read a poem and an excerpt from a short story and then write an essay. You may make notes as you read the selections.

Your Task: Read the poem "A Dream Deferred" and the selection from "Araby." Then write an essay in which you

- Discuss the theme of disappointed hopes as it is presented in both works

- Show how specific literary elements and specific literary techniques help to convey the theme of each piece

ANSWER: did

In your essay, be sure to

- Discuss the theme of disappointed hopes revealed in both selections
- Show how specific literary elements and specific literary techniques help to convey the theme in each selection
- Organize your ideas in a unified and coherent manner
- Follow the conventions of standard written English

Writing Prompt 2

Texts: Excerpt from the short story "The Good Dead," by Pearl S. Buck, and the poem "The Bean Eaters," by Gwendolyn Brooks

Directions to Students: For this part of the test, you will read a poem and an excerpt from a short story and then write an essay. You may make notes as you read the selections.

Your Task: Read the poem "The Bean Eaters" and the selection from "The Good Dead." Then write an essay in which you

- Analyze the difference in how the characters in each work experience old age
- Show how specific literary elements and specific literary techniques help to convey these differences

In your essay, be sure to

- Discuss the conflicting experiences of old age revealed in the selections
- Show how specific literary elements and specific literary techniques help to convey these differences
- Organize your ideas in a unified and coherent manner
- Follow the conventions of standard written English

B. Project

Work with other students in a small group to write two prompts for Part 2 of the Comprehensive English Examination. Follow the format for prompts shown in this lesson. Base your prompts on poetry and prose that you have studied in class or that you find in anthologies in the library.

Lesson 3.3

Literary Genres, Elements, and Techniques

File   Activity   Edit   Help

See Movie
Call Friend
Listen to CDs
Read Lesson 3.3
Go to Concert
Go Shopping

Genres of Literature

In Part 3 of the Comprehensive Examination in English, you will be asked to write about a couple of literary selections. You will most likely be given one prose piece and one poem to read. The prose piece will most likely be part or all of some **narrative,** or piece that tells a story. Make sure that you are familiar with the types, or **genres,** of narrative and poem described in the following charts:

 Types of Prose Narrative

1. **Short Story.** A **short story** is a brief work of fiction. The prose selection included in the Pretest for this unit is part of a short story by the Russian writer Leo Tolstoy.

2. **Narrative Poem.** A **narrative poem** is verse that tells a story. Ballads are narrative poems divided into four-line or six-line stanzas.

3. **Autobiographical Essay/Memoir.** In an **autobiographical essay** or **memoir,** a writer tells a true story from his or her own life.

4. **Biographical Essay.** In a **biographical essay,** a writer tells a true story from someone else's life.

5. **Narrative Personal Essay.** A **narrative personal essay** is a short nonfiction work about a single topic and may be autobiographical or contain autobiographical elements. Usually, a narrative personal essay is written to make a specific point and uses a true autobiographical story to illustrate the point.

ANSWER: May

6. **Journal** or **Diary.** A **journal** or **diary** is a day-to-day account and may be true (like *The Diary of Anne Frank*) or fictional (like *The Diary of Adrian Mole*, by Sue Townsend, or *The Diary of Adam and Eve*, by Mark Twain). Book-length journals or diaries are often excerpted.

7. **Myth.** A **myth** is a story dealing with a god or goddess. Often myths explain the origins of natural phenomena. For example, the Greek myth of Arachne explains the origins of spiders.

8. **Legend.** A **legend** is a story about a hero or heroine. Legends may be partially or wholly true. The legends about King Arthur are almost entirely fictional.

9. **Tall Tale.** A **tall tale** is a story with wildly exaggerated characters and events.

10. **Anecdote.** An **anecdote** is a very brief story, often true, told to make a point.

Types of Poem

1. **Narrative Poem.** A **narrative poem** is verse that tells a story.

2. **Dramatic Poem.** A **dramatic poem** is verse that presents the speech of one or more characters in a dramatic situation. In a **dramatic monologue,** one character speaks. In a **dramatic dialogue,** two characters speak.

3. **Lyric Poem.** A **lyric poem** is short, highly musical verse that expresses the thoughts and emotions of a speaker.

Notice that narratives can be fiction or nonfiction. A work of **fiction** tells about imaginary people and characters. A work of **nonfiction,** such as a memoir or biography, tells about real people and characters. Another genre, or kind of literature, that you might encounter on the exam is **satire,** in which a writer pokes fun at someone or something. A satire can be in poetry or prose. There are many other genres of literature, including stage plays, screenplays, fables, and proverbs, but the ones listed above are those most likely to be used in Part 3 of the exam.

GUM: Don't ask (anything, nothing).

Literary Elements and Techniques

Notice that the Your Task portion of the writing prompt on page 116 requires you to refer in your essay to specific literary elements and techniques used in the selections. Therefore, it is extremely important that you know the major elements and techniques and that you be able to recognize them in works of literature. The charts on the following pages explain elements and techniques found in literature in general and in poetry in particular. Elements and techniques peculiar to narratives (stories) will be treated in Lesson 3.5. Study the examples given in the chart, and make sure that you understand each of these elements and techniques. Doing so will help you considerably to pass Part 3 of the exam.

 Elements and Techniques Found in All Genres of Literature

1. **Image.** An **image** is a word or phrase that names something that can be seen, heard, touched, tasted, or smelled. A collection or group of images is called **imagery.** Example: Ice covered the ground, and a cold wind whistled through the tree limbs.

2. **Setting.** The **setting** is the time and place in which a work of literature occurs. Setting is created by details describing elements such as costumes and scenery.

3. **Mood.** The **mood** is the emotional quality of a literary work. Mood is created by imagery, word choice, events, and other literary elements. Adjectives that describe moods include gloomy, sad, joyful, reflective, suspenseful, and horrific.

4. **Subject.** The **subject** is the matter that a work is about. Common subjects of literary works include childhood, diversity, wonder, aging, nature, individuality, love, justice, discrimination, struggle, death, courage, hope, determination, loyalty, and freedom.

5. **Theme.** A **theme** is a main idea in a literary work. For example, a work on the subject of aging might have as its theme the idea that older people can still be young and fresh in their thinking.

6. **Character.** A **character** is a figure who takes part in the action of a literary work.

7. **Suspense.** **Suspense** is a feeling of curiosity or expectation, often tinged with anxiety, created by questions about what the outcome will be in a literary work.

8. **Tone.** **Tone** is the attitude adopted by the speaker, narrator, or author of a literary work toward the subject or the reader of the work.

ANSWER: anything

9. **Voice,** or **Style.** A writer's **voice,** or **style,** is the sum of all the characteristics that make his or her work sound unique. Hemingway was famous for a style that made use of short, simple sentences with few embellishments. Faulkner was famous for a style that made use of long, complicated sentences full of flourishes like alliteration and unusual diction.

10. **Flashbacks** and **Foreshadowing.** A **flashback** takes the reader to an earlier part of a story. **Foreshadowing** hints about events to come.

Figurative Language, or **Figures of Speech**
(expressions with a meaning other than or beyond the literal)

11. **Hyperbole.** A **hyperbole** is an exaggeration for effect. Example: I will love you until the end of time.

12. **Irony. Irony** is a contradiction, such as a difference between appearance and reality or a difference between what is said and what is meant. In the selection from "The Death of Iván Illych," it is ironic that Illych should believe that all people must die but not be willing to believe that he must eventually die.

13. **Metaphor.** A **metaphor** is a figure of speech in which one thing is described as if it were another. Example: My love is a red, red rose.

14. **Simile.** A **simile** is a type of metaphor, a comparison using *like* or *as.* Example: My love is like a red, red rose.

15. **Apostrophe.** An **apostrophe** is words addressed directly to a person or thing, often in exclamatory sentences. Example: Milton! Thou shouldst be living at this hour!

16. **Personification. Personification** is a figure of speech in which a nonhuman thing is described as though it were human. Example: The old car coughed, cried out once, and then gave up the ghost. Personification can occur in an apostrophe if a speaker or character directly addresses an inanimate object. Example: O wild West Wind, thou breath of Autumn's being!

17. **Symbol.** A **symbol** is something that stands both for itself and for something beyond itself. Roses are traditional symbols of love and beauty. A dove is a traditional symbol of peace.

18. **Synesthesia. Synesthesia** is a figure of speech in which two different senses are combined. Example: Jack wore a noisy red sweater.

19. **Understatement.** An **understatement** is an ironic expression in which something of importance is emphasized by being spoken of as though it were not important. Example: The Emperor was dealing with a few minor matters, like war on his borders and food riots in the streets of his cities.

GUM: Everyone went to (his own home, their own homes). Literary Genres, Elements, and Techniques

Rhetorical Techniques (unusual but literal uses of language)

20. **Antithesis.** An **antithesis** is a strong contrast between two ideas. Examples: a. I expected joy. I found despair. b. cold hands, warm heart

21. **Parallelism. Parallelism** is the use of similar grammatical forms to give items equal weight, as in Lincoln's line "of the people, by the people, for the people."

22. **Repetition. Repetition** is the use, again, of any element, such as a sound, word, phrase, clause, or sentence. Example: Rows of men marched away. Rows of men raised their rifles. Rows of men were mown down like winter wheat.

23. **Rhetorical Question.** A **rhetorical question** is one asked for effect but not meant to be answered because the answer is clear. Example: Are we not Americans? Will we not stand up against challenges to our freedom?

Techniques Involving Sound (commonly but not exclusively found in poetry)

24. **Alliteration. Alliteration** is the repetition of initial consonant sounds. Example: Nature to all things fixed the limits fit.

25. **Onomatopoeia. Onomatopoeia** is the use of words or phrases that sound like the things that they describe. Examples: buzz, chop, clatter, mumble, clank, meow

26. **Rhythm. Rhythm** is the pattern of beats, or stressed and unstressed syllables, in a line. The following line is made up of unstressed syllables (∪) followed by stressed syllables (/):

∪ / ∪ / ∪ / ∪ / ∪ /

Is this the face that launched a thousand ships?

"A Birthday," by Christina Rossetti

My heart is like a singing bird
   Whose nest is in a watered shoot;
My heart is like an apple tree
   Whose boughs are bent with thickset fruit;
My heart is like a rainbow shell
   That paddles in a halcyon sea;
My heart is gladder than all these
   Because my love is come to me.

Raise me a dais of silk and down;
   Hang it with vair and purple dyes;
Carve it in doves and pomegranates,
   And peacocks with a hundred eyes;
Work in it gold and silver grapes,
   In leaves and silver fleurs-de-lys;
Because the birthday of my life
   Is come, my love is come to me.

ANSWER: his own home

Rhyme Scheme (the pattern of rhymes in a poem)

1. **Rhymed verse** is poetry with a regular rhyme scheme.

2. **End rhyme** is rhyming at the ends of lines, as in

   For never was a story of more w<u>oe</u>
   Than this of Juliet and her Rome<u>o</u>.

3. **Internal rhyme** is rhyming within lines, as in "I s<u>ee</u> a bus<u>y</u> bumbleb<u>ee</u>."

4. **Slant rhyme** is a near rhyme, as in "What did the w<u>ind</u> / Seek to f<u>ind</u>?"

Meter (the rhythmical pattern in a poem)

5. **Free verse** is poetry that does not have a set pattern of rhythm or rhyme.

6. **Metrical verse** is poetry with a regular rhythmic pattern.

Stanza Form

7. A **stanza** is a group of lines in a poem.

8. A **couplet** is a two-line stanza.

9. A **triplet,** or **tercet,** is a three-line stanza.

10. A **quatrain** is a four-line stanza.

11. A **quintain** is a five-line stanza.

12. A **sestet** is a six-line stanza.

13. A **heptastich** is a seven-line stanza.

14. An **octave** is an eight-line stanza.

15. A **sonnet** is a poem with fourteen lines having any of a number of different standard rhyme schemes.

File   Activity   Edit   Help

See Movie
Call Friend
Listen to CDs
Do Activities, Lesson 3.3
Go to Concert
Go Shopping

A. Recalling the Lesson

Reread "Death, Be Not Proud," on page 117, and "A Birthday," on page 130. Then do the following:

1. Find an example of apostrophe in "Death, Be Not Proud."

2. Explain why "Death, Be Not Proud" can be called a sonnet.

3. Tell what kinds of poem "Death, Be Not Proud" and "A Birthday" are—narrative, dramatic, or lyric.

4. Find three similes in "A Birthday."

5. Find an example of personification in "Death, Be Not Proud."

6. Answer these questions: Is "A Birthday" free verse? rhymed verse? metrical verse?

7. Find two examples of metaphor in "Death, Be Not Proud."

8. Find one example of irony in "Death, Be Not Proud."

9. Find examples of repetition in "A Birthday."

10. Find one example of alliteration in "Death, Be Not Proud" and one example in "A Birthday."

11. Explain the tone of the speaker in each of these poems.

12. What is the stanza form of "A Birthday"?

13. In line 4 of "A Birthday," the speaker mentions fruit. Of what might this fruit be a symbol?

14. What is the theme of "A Birthday"? of "Death, Be Not Proud"?

B. Project

Work with other students in a small group to find or write examples of each of the literary techniques described in this lesson.

ANSWER: Those

Lesson 3.4

Reading a Lyric Poem

See Movie
Call Friend
Listen to CDs
Read Lesson 3.4
Go to Concert
Go Shopping

Steps in Reading a Lyric Poem

In Part 3 of the Comprehensive Examination in English, you will be asked to write about a couple of literary selections. Usually, at least one of the selections will be a poem. In most cases, the poem will be a **lyric**—a short poem that expresses a speaker's emotions and ideas in concrete, precise, musical language.

Students usually have more problems with poetry than with any other kind of literature. However, reading poetry doesn't have to be difficult. If you take the right approach, you'll find that reading poetry isn't that difficult after all. In fact, reading poetry (and writing it) can be a lot of fun.

In the Renaissance era, four to five hundred years ago, well-to-do, powerful people—kings and queens, lords and ladies—often sent lyric poems to one another. These poems were like personal letters. Today, people still sometimes write lyric poems for the same purpose. In fact, the simplest way to think about a lyric poem is to consider it a kind of letter from the poem's speaker. Like a letter, the poem tells us what someone thinks and feels. Let's look at an example:

Have You Forgotten?

   by James Worley

The curiosity of cats, observed,
can enable men to retrieve infancy:
some sights and sounds and the movements bridging them
entice the kitten and the child alike:
the drip of faucets, the slide of sinkside streams,
the play of light reflected to a wall,
the crumpled paper breathing on the floor—
have you forgotten? watch a cat! return!

GUM: We (haven't, have) no books by Mr. Poe.

When reading a poem, don't be put off by the division of the poem into lines. Remember that most poems, like stories, are written in sentences. Don't worry about the line breaks. Simply read each sentence in the poem separately, and try to **paraphrase** it, or put it into your own words. Let's try this with James Worley's poem.

The first lines of the poem say, "The curiosity of cats, observed, / can enable men to retrieve infancy." In other words, if we observe, or watch, how curious cats are, we can become like children again. The second statement in the poem is, "[S]ome sights and sounds and the movements bridging them / entice the kitten and the child alike." In other words, both children and kittens are enticed, or attracted, by some sights, sounds, and movements. The poem then presents a  list of some things that kittens and children are attracted to: dripping faucets, streams of water sliding down the sides of sinks, light reflected and "playing" on a wall, crumpled paper "breathing" on the floor. The speaker then asks the reader a question, "[H]ave you forgotten?" Next the poem promises that if you watch a cat, you can "return," or go back. In other words, if you do not remember what it was like to be a child, if you do not remember how to take joy in the tiny, little events occurring all around you, simply watch a cat, and you'll remember a time when you, too, enjoyed all the little miracles in life.

The first step in understanding a poem, then, is to paraphrase it, or put its sentences into your own words. Sometimes you will encounter words in poems that you don't understand. For example, you might not have known the meaning of the word *entice* in line 4 of "Have You Forgotten?" When reading a poem on your own, you can look up such difficult words in a dictionary. When you are reading a poem during the Comprehensive Exam, you won't be able to refer to a dictionary, so you will have to figure out such words from context.

The next step toward understanding a lyric poem is to ask yourself about the speaker and about the subject. Imagine that you are an anthropologist from the year 2225 and that you have just dug up a box. In the box you have found a journal, and in

ANSWER: have

the journal you have found the poem "Have You Forgotten?" What does the poem tell you about its speaker? Who was this person? What was this person speaking about? What did this person think and feel? To answer questions like this, you need to look for clues in the poem. Make a list of things that the poem reveals about the speaker:

The speaker . . .

—is interested in cats

—is probably a man because of the reference, in line 2, to "men"

—must be older, no longer a child, because he speaks about "retriev[ing] infancy"

—thinks that people ought to observe cats

—thinks that observing cats will make it possible for people to "retrieve infancy"

—seems to feel that retrieving infancy, or becoming like a child again, is a good thing

—is very observant about little things (dripping faucets, light playing on the wall, etc.)

—wants us to watch cats so that we can remember what we were like when we were children and full of curiosity ourselves

After you have paraphrased the poem, have identified the subject, and have listed the characteristics, interests, ideas, and feelings of the speaker, you are ready to state the poem's **theme,** or main idea. In a lyric poem, the theme is the main message that the speaker wants to communicate:

Theme: Watching cats can help people to regain the sort of curiosity—wonder about and interest in ordinary things—that they had when they were children.

Finally, you can make a list of the special literary techniques used in the poem. These techniques include such features as rhythm, rhyme, alliteration, metaphors, and similes. If you have forgotten what any of these terms mean, go back to the previous lesson and review them.

Techniques in the Poem

Alliteration

—<u>c</u>uriosity of <u>c</u>ats

—<u>s</u>ink<u>s</u>ide

VOC: Words with the root *graph,* meaning "to write."

Rhyme

—sl<u>ide</u> of sink<u>side</u>

Metaphor

—movements connecting sights and
sounds are compared to bridges

Personification

—light is said to "play"

—crumpled paper, moving on the
floor, is described as "breathing"

Finally, look over your list of techniques and ask yourself how these reinforce the poem's meaning. The alliteration and rhyme in the poem make it more musical and thus more memorable. Describing the movements as bridges reinforces the idea that watching a cat can be a kind of bridge back to one's own childhood. Personifying the light and the paper on the floor tell us that if we exercise our curiosity, then little things in the world will seem more interesting. They will "come alive."

Taking Notes on a Poem During the Exam

If one of the works that you are asked to read during Part 3 of the exam is a poem, begin by reading the poem through two or three times without taking notes. Then, on your scrap paper, take notes on the poem, following the steps outlined in the chart at the top of the next page.

Important: Do not skip the notetaking stage. It is extremely important that you take the time to read the poem carefully and take notes on it before you start to write your essay. Your notes will supply the material that you will use in the essay that you are going to write. To do well on this part of the exam, you must practice this notetaking procedure many times, so that it becomes second nature to you. When an artist paints a picture, he or she first begins with a good sketch. When a person writes an essay, he or she should begin with good notes.

ANSWER: graph, graphic, telegraph, monograph

1. First, paraphrase the poem. That is, restate its sentences in your own words.

2. Second, look for clues in the poem that tell you what the speaker is speaking about—his or her subject—and list that subject.

3. Third, based on clues in the poem, make a list telling what the poem reveals about the speaker's interests, ideas, and feelings.

4. Fourth, state the main idea, or theme, that the speaker of the poem is expressing.

5. Fifth, make a list of special literary techniques used in the poem.

6. Sixth, make a few notes to yourself about how these techniques reinforce the poem's theme.

Paraphrase
— If we watch how curious cats are, we can become like children again
— Both children and kittens are attracted by some sights, sounds and movements
— List of sights, sounds, and movements
— If you've forgotten what it was like to be a child, you can remember by watching a cat

Subject: Watching Cats

The Speaker
— is interested in cats
— is probably a man (line 2: "man")
— must be older, no longer child
— thinks people should observe cats
— thinks observing cats will help person to retrieve infancy
— seems to feel that retrieving infancy is a good thing
— is observant himself

Theme: Watching cats can help people to regain curiosity— the wonder and interest in ordinary things — that they had when they were children

Techniques

Alliteration
— curiosity of cats
— sinkside

Rhyme
— slide of sinkside

Metaphor
— movements like bridges

Personification
— light "plays"
— paper "breathing"

GUM: (Its, It's) a long way to Tipperary.

Poems for Practice

Brahma[1]

by Ralph Waldo Emerson

If the red slayer thinks he slays,
    Or if the slain think he is slain,
They know not well the subtle ways
    I keep, and pass, and turn again.

Far or forgot to me is near;
    Shadow and sunlight are the same;
The vanished gods to me appear;
    And one to me are shame and fame.

They reckon ill who leave me out;
    When me they fly, I am the wings;
I am the doubter and the doubt,
    And I the hymn the Brahmin[2] sings.

The strong gods[3] pine for my abode,
    And pine in vain the sacred Seven;
But thou, meek lover of the good!
    Find me, and turn thy back[4] on heaven.

[1] **Brahma.** Supreme god of the Hindu religion. Emerson, a Unitarian minister and one of the greatest of the nineteenth-century American poets, was strongly influenced by Hindu sacred texts and philosophy.

[2] **Brahmin.** Member of the highest caste of Hindu society, the priestly caste

[3] **strong gods.** Lesser gods. Hindus are polytheistic, believing in many gods subordinate to and part of the one supreme god.

[4] **turn thy back.** According to Hindu philosophy, all things, good and bad, are part of Brahma, and people should therefore embrace life in all its complexity. Emerson's line suggests turning away from simplistic ideas and embracing a more inclusive spirituality.

Ralph Waldo Emerson

ANSWER: It's

Alone

by Edgar Allan Poe

From childhood's hour I have not been
As others were—I have not seen
As others saw—I could not bring
My passions from a common spring—
From the same source I have not taken
My sorrow—I could not awaken
My heart to joy at the same tone—
And all I lov'd— I lov'd alone—
Then—in my childhood—in the dawn
Of a most stormy life—was drawn
From ev'ry depth of good and ill
The mystery which binds me still—
From the torrent, or the fountain—
From the red cliff of the mountain—
From the sun that round me roll'd
In its autumn tint of gold—
From the lightning in the sky
As it pass'd me flying by—
From the thunder, and the storm—
And the cloud that took the form
(When the rest of Heaven was blue)
Of a demon in my view—

Edgar Allan Poe

File Activity Edit Help

   See Movie
   Call Friend
   Listen to CDs
   Do Activities, Lesson 3.4
   Go to Concert
   Go Shopping

A. Practicing Your Skills

Choose one poem from the last two pages and do the following:

1. First, paraphrase the poem. That is, restate its sentences in your own words.

2. Second, look for clues in the poem that tell you what the speaker is speaking about—his or her subject, and list that subject.

3. Third, based on clues in the poem, make a list telling what the poem reveals about the speaker's interests, ideas, and feelings.

4. Fourth, state the main idea, or theme, that the speaker of the poem is expressing.

5. Fifth, make a list of special literary techniques used in the poem.

6. Sixth, make a few notes to yourself about how these techniques reinforce the poem's theme.

B. Writing

Write a paragraph explaining the theme, or main idea, of the poem that you chose for Exercise A. Begin your paragraph with a topic sentence that states the title, author, and theme of the poem, like this:

> The theme of James Worley's poem "Have You Forgotten" is that by observing the playful curiosity of cats, we can remember the wonder that we felt about the world when we were very young.

After your topic sentence, write at least five or six additional sentences that present evidence from the poem that supports your topic sentence. Use **transitions,** such as *first, second, third, then, next, finally, in conclusion*, and so on, to connect your ideas.

   ANSWER: telegraph, telephoto, telephone, telegraphy

Lesson 3.5

Reading a Narrative

See Movie
Call Friend
Listen to CDs
Read Lesson 3.5
Go to Concert
Go Shopping

Understanding Narratives

There is a good chance that more than one of the selections that you will read for Parts 3 and 4 of the Comprehensive Exam will be a short narrative. A **narrative** is any literary work that tells a story. Good possibilities for narratives on the exam include selections from short stories, very brief short stories, or selections from autobiographies or memoirs. Although these kinds of narrative differ in important respects, you can follow the same steps when reading them and taking notes on them during the exam. That's because all narratives have at least some elements in common. The next section of this lesson will describe some of the elements that are common to narratives, but first, we shall look at a sample narrative to be used as a basis for the discussion.

The Story of an Hour

by Kate Chopin

Because Mrs. Mallard[1] was afflicted with heart trouble, great care was taken to break to her as gently as possible the news of her husband's death.

It was her sister Josephine who told her, in broken sentences; veiled hints that revealed in half concealing. Her husband's friend Richards was there, too, near her. It was he who had been in the newspaper office when intelligence of the railroad disaster was received, with Brently Mallard's name leading the list of "killed." He had only taken the time to assure himself of its truth by a second telegram, and had hastened to forestall any less careful, less tender friend in bearing the sad message.

---

[1] **Mallard.** A common kind of wild duck, known for its tendency to mate for a lifetime

GUM: The boss says that I (can, may) go home early.

She did not hear the story as many women have heard the same, with a paralyzed inability to accept its significance. She wept at once, with sudden, wild abandonment, in her sister's arms. When the storm of grief had spent itself she went away to her room alone. She would have no one follow her.

There stood, facing the open window, a comfortable, roomy armchair. Into this she sank, pressed down by a physical exhaustion that haunted her body and seemed to reach into her soul.

She could see in the open square before her house the tops of trees that were all aquiver with the new spring life. The delicious breath of rain was in the air. In the street below, a peddler was crying his wares. The notes of a distant song which someone was singing reached her faintly, and countless sparrows were twittering in the eaves.

There were patches of blue sky showing here and there through the clouds that had met and piled one above the other in the west facing her window.

She sat with her head thrown back upon the cushion of the chair, quite motionless except when a sob came up into her throat and shook her, as a child who has cried itself to sleep continues to sob in its dreams.

She was young, with a fair, calm face, whose lines bespoke repression and even a certain strength. But now there was a dull stare in her eyes, whose gaze was fixed away off yonder on one of those patches of blue sky. It was not a glance of reflection but rather indicated a suspension of intelligent thought.

There was something coming to her and she was waiting for it, fearfully. What was it? She did not know: it was too subtle and elusive to name. But she felt it, creeping out of the sky, reaching toward her through the sounds, the scents, the color that filled the air.

ANSWER: may

Now her bosom rose and fell tumultuously. She was beginning to recognize this thing that was approaching to possess her, and she was striving to beat it back with her will—as powerless as her two white slender hands would have been.

When she abandoned herself, a little whispered word escaped her slightly parted lips. She said it over and over under her breath: "free, free, free!" The vacant stare and the look of terror that had followed it went from her eyes. They stayed keen and bright. Her pulses beat fast, and the coursing blood warmed and relaxed every inch of her body.

She did not stop to ask if it were or were not a monstrous joy that held her. A clear and exalted perception enabled her to dismiss the suggestion as trivial.

She knew that she would weep again when she saw the kind, tender hands folded in death; the face that had never looked save with love upon her, fixed and gray and dead. But she saw beyond that bitter moment a long procession of years to come that would belong to her absolutely. And she opened and spread her arms out to them in welcome.

There would be no one to live for her during those coming years; she would live for herself. There would be no powerful will bending hers in that blind persistence with which men and women believe they have a right to impose a private will upon a fellow creature. A kind intention or a cruel intention made the act seem no less a crime as she looked upon it in that brief moment of illumination.

And yet she had loved him—sometimes. Often she had not. What did it matter! What could love, the unsolved mystery, count for in face of this possession of self-assertion which she suddenly recognized as the strongest impulse of her being!

"Free! Body and soul free!" she kept whispering.

GUM: There were (less, fewer) snow days this year.

Josephine was kneeling before the closed door with her lips to the keyhole, imploring for admission. "Louise, open the door! I beg; open the door—you will make yourself ill. What are you doing, Louise? For heaven's sake open the door."

"Go away. I am not making myself ill." No; she was drinking in a very elixir of life through that open window.

Her fancy was running riot along those days ahead of her. Spring days, and summer days, and all sorts of days that would be her own. She breathed a quick prayer that life might be long. It was only yesterday she had thought with a shudder that life might be long.

She arose at length and opened the door to her sister's importunities. There was a feverish triumph in her eyes, and she carried herself unwittingly like a goddess of Victory. She clasped her sister's waist, and together they descended the stairs. Richards stood waiting for them at the bottom.

Someone was opening the front door with a latchkey. It was Brently Mallard who entered, a little travel-stained, composedly carrying his gripsack and umbrella. He had been far from the scene of the accident and did not know there had been one. He stood amazed at Josephine's piercing cry; at Richards's quick motion to screen him from the view of his wife.

But Richards was too late.

When the doctors came they said she had died of heart disease—of joy that kills.

ANSWER: fewer

The Elements of a Narrative

The following chart describes some elements common to all narratives, from narrative poems to short stories to memoirs or autobiographies. Make sure that you understand the terms on the chart, can identify these in a narrative, and can refer to them when discussing and writing about narratives.

The Parts of a Narrative

1. The **setting** is the time and place in which the action occurs.

2. The **mood** is the overall emotional quality of the selection or of a part of the selection (awed, melancholic, hopeful, etc.).

3. The **tone** is the attitude adopted by the author or the narrator toward the subject or the reader of the work (joyful, sad, frightened, excited, anxious, urgent, satirical, etc.).

4. The **narrator** is the person telling the story. In stories told from the **first-person point of view**, the narrator uses words such as *I* and *we* and may participate in the action of the story. In stories told from the **third-person point of view,** the narrator uses words such as *he*, *she*, and *they* and does not take part in the action of the story.

5. The **characters** are the figures who take part in the action of the narrative. These include **main characters,** such as the protagonist and antagonist, and **minor characters** who play smaller roles. A character who changes is known as a **dynamic character**. A character who does not change is known as a **static character.** A **flat, stock,** or **stereotypical** character is one who is one-dimensional and not fully developed.

6. The **protagonist** is the main character in the selection. Usually, the main character experiences some conflict, or struggle, and goes through some important change.

7. Some stories have an **antagonist,** a person or force that struggles with the protagonist.

8. The **central conflict** is the major struggle experienced by the protagonist. This conflict may be **external** (between the character and an outside force) or **internal** (within the character).

9. The **plot** is the series of events in the narrative. The plot begins with an **inciting incident,** which introduces the central conflict. The inciting incident is followed by the **rising action,** in which the central conflict is developed. The **climax** is the high point of interest or suspense in the story. The **crisis,** or **turning point,** is a point in the story at which something decisive happens to determine the future course of events in the narrative and the working out of the conflict. The events that occur after the turning point are called the **falling action.** The falling action ends with the **resolution,** the point in the story at which the central conflict is resolved.

10. **Motive. A motive** is a reason that a character acts in a certain way. **Motivation** is what impels the character. For instance,the motivation might be money and the motive might be greed.

GUM: The cat can't get (in, into) the goldfish bowl.

Taking Notes on a Narrative During the Exam

Bear in mind that a given narrative might not contain all of these parts. Consider, for example, the selection from "The Death of Iván Illych," which is one of the readings for the Pretest (Lesson 3.1). Since this is just a selection from the middle of a short story, it does not contain some of the elements of short stories, such as the inciting incident, a climax, and a resolution of the central conflict.

The key thing to remember about narratives is that almost all of them center upon a **central conflict,** or struggle. Usually, by facing this central conflict, the main character grows and changes in some way. The character learns something, and what the character learns becomes the **theme,** the main idea or central point of the narrative.

As you read the selection, bear in mind what the exam prompt asks you to look for, and note key elements of the narrative related to the subject of the composition that you are supposed to write. The writing prompt for the Pretest for this unit asks you to contrast the attitudes toward death represented in two selections. Therefore, while reading the selection from "The Death of Iván Illych," you should have looked for literary elements related to the central character's attitude toward death.

A sample of one student's notes about the selection is given on the following page. Notice the following characteristics of these notes:

1. The student has used <u>literary terms</u>, such as *protagonist, central conflict, tone, irony,* and *theme,* throughout her notes.

2. The student has paid particular attention to aspects of the selection that deal with <u>the subject in the writing prompt</u> (death).

3. The student's notes include <u>quotations from the selection</u> as examples to back up the points made in her notes.

4. The notes contain a one-sentence <u>summary</u> of what the selection reveals about the subject of the writing prompt (the attitude of the character toward death).

Important: Make sure that your notes on the prose selections contain at least these parts! You will need at least this much information to write your response to the exam question. As you can see, knowing the literary terms given in this lesson and in Lesson 3.3 is **extremely important.** Make sure that you understand these terms and have practiced writing notes that contain all of the elements mentioned above before you take the exam!

ANSWER: into

Maria Robinson
Thurs., Feb. 12

"The Death of Iván Illych," Leo Tolstoy

Protagonist—Iván Illych
  —Conflict: cannot accept fact that he is
    dying
  —Illych's attitude: disbelieving and afraid
    —"He refused . . . to give admittance to
      the thought"
    —"[H]e felt nothing but despair"
    —"It makes no sense. No sense at all."

Literary techniques
  —Personification
    —Death is an "unwelcome guest" who is
      "unacceptable in the parlor of his consciousness"
    —Describes death as "a highwayman," as "a thief,"
      someone "knocking at the door of his consciousness,"
      "a bill collector," and "a murderer"
  —Irony
    —Illych is a public prosecutor, used to logical arguments
      in court
    —Illych remembers argument about death from a
      logic book
    —But Illych can't accept the logical truth that he, too, must die

Theme: Difficulty of facing one's own death

Attitude toward death in selection: disbelieving, horrified

File   Activity   Edit   Help

See Movie
Call Friend
Listen to CDs
Do Activities, Lesson 3.5
Go to Concert
Go Shopping

A. Understanding the Elements and Techniques Used in Narratives

Using information from this lesson, fill in the blanks in the following story maps for the selection from "The Death of Iván Illych" (pages 118 and 119) and for "The Story of an Hour" (pages 141–44).

Story Map

Title of Story: _____"The Death of Iván Illych"_____

Author of Story: _____

Setting:

Images, details that reveal time and place: _____

_____

_____

_____

Protagonist:

_____

Details that reveal the character of the protagonist: _____

_____

_____

ANSWER: President

Conflict:

Central conflict in the selection:_____

_____

_____

Is the central conflict internal or external? ☐ internal ☐ external

Literary Techniques:

Irony:_____

_____

_____

Personification:_____

_____

_____

Theme:

What does the selection tell us about some people's reactions to the idea of dying?

_____

_____

_____

_____

_____

_____

_____

Story Map

Title of Story: _"The Story of an Hour"_

Author of Story: _____

Characters:

Protagonist: _____

Other characters: _____

_____

_____

Setting:

Images, details that reveal time and place: _____

_____

_____

Influence of the setting on the main character: _____

_____

_____

Literary Techniques:

Meaning of symbols:

   window: _____

   spring: _____

Irony: _____

_____

_____

ANSWER: French

Plot of the Story:

Inciting Incident:_____

_____

Central Conflict:_____

_____

Rising Action:_____

_____

Turning Point:_____

_____

Resolution:_____

_____

Is the central conflict internal or external?   ☐ internal   ☐ external

How does the protagonist change in the course of the story?

_____

_____

_____

Theme:

What does the story tell us about feelings of repression experienced by married women in the nineteenth century?

_____

_____

_____

_____

_____

B. Taking Notes on a Narrative

Imagine that the subject of the writing prompt for Part 3 of the exam is "attitudes toward love." Take notes on "The Story of an Hour," using a rough outline form or another graphic organizer. Make sure that you follow these guidelines when taking your notes:

1. Use <u>literary terms</u>, such as *protagonist*, *central conflict*, *tone*, *irony*, *symbol*, and *theme*.
2. Respond to aspects of the selection related to <u>the subject in the writing prompt</u>.
3. Use <u>quotations from the selection</u> as examples to back up the points that you make.
4. Include a one-sentence <u>summary</u> of the attitude that the central character comes to have, in the course of the story, toward love (specifically, the attitude that she comes to have in regard to not having her husband around anymore). Hint: Which is more important to the character in this story, love or freedom?

C. Planning an Essay Contrasting Two Works

Note the ways in which "A Birthday" and "The Story of an Hour" differ in their portrayal of a character's attitude toward her romantic partner. Consider mood, imagery or symbolism, and theme. Fill in the chart below with examples from each selection that show different attitudes toward love.

COMPARISON AND CONTRAST: ATTITUDES TOWARD LOVE	
"A Birthday"	**"The Story of an Hour"**

ANSWER: Jess's

Lesson 3.6

Using Quotations as Evidence in Your Writing

See Movie
Call Friend
Listen to CDs
Read Lesson 3.6
Go to Concert
Go Shopping

Quoting Versus Paraphrasing or Summarizing

Whenever you write about works of literature, it is important that you use **evidence**—specific facts from the selection that support the statements that you make. Each body paragraph for an essay about literature should have:

- a **topic sentence**—a general statement about the work or works
- **elaboration** —several sentences giving specific examples from the work or works

There are three kinds of evidence that you can present from literary works. You can **quote** from the work, using words and phrases picked up **verbatim,** or word-for-word, from the text; you can **paraphrase** parts of the work, putting them into your own words; or you can **summarize,** restating all or part of the work briefly, in a few of your own words.

Consider the following passage from "The Story of an Hour":

> She did not hear the story as many women have heard the same, with a paralyzed inability to accept its significance. She wept at once, with sudden, wild abandonment, in her sister's arms. When the storm of grief had spent itself she went away to her room alone. She would have no one follow her.

Here is an example in which a student paraphrases, or restates, this part of the story in her own words:

> When Mrs. Mallard first hears about the death of her husband, she
> reacts strongly, crying in the arms of her sister. The narrator describes
> Mrs. Mallard's reaction as being like a storm. After her initial reaction,
> Mrs. Mallard goes off to her room by herself.

GUM: We read (Tolstoys, Tolstoy's) *War and Peace.*

Here is an example in which a student uses quotations from the work:

> When Mrs. Mallard first hears about the death of her husband, she
> reacts strongly. She weeps "at once, with sudden, wild abandonment,
> in her sister's arms." She experiences what the narrator metaphorically
> calls a "storm of grief" and then goes "away to her room alone."

Notice that any words that you use verbatim from a selection must be placed within quotation marks.

Guidelines for Quoting

Follow the guidelines on this chart when quoting from literary works:

 Incorporating Quotations into Your Writing

1. Use quotation marks around direct quotations but not around paraphrases.

2. When quoting three lines or fewer from the selection, run the quotation into your paragraph, as in the example at the top of this page. When quoting more than three lines, set the quotation off from the left and right margins, single-space the quotation, and do not use quotation marks, as in this example:

> The mood of the protagonist changes dramatically halfway through the story. At first
> she is not even aware, herself, of what is happening to her. She just knows that she is
> beginning to feel something different:
>
> > There was something coming to her and she was waiting for it, fearfully.
> > What was it? She did not know: it was too subtle and elusive to name. But she
> > felt it, creeping out of the sky, reaching toward her through the sounds, the
> > scents, the color that filled the air.
>
> The change coming over her seems to be related to the spring scene outside her window.
> Spring, of course, is a traditional symbol of rebirth and awakening, and it is just such a
> rebirth that she is starting to feel.

3. When quoting more than one line from a poem, use a slash mark (/) with spaces on either side to separate the lines. Capitalize the quotation exactly as in the source.

> The speaker of "A Birthday" has also experienced a rebirth, but of a different
> kind. She says that she is overjoyed "Because the birthday of [her] life / Is come."

4. Make sure that quotations fit grammatically into your sentences. If you need to change a verb or a pronoun to make it agree, as in the above example, place the changed, nonverbatim material in brackets [ ].

ANSWER: Tolstoy's

5. Enclose quotations within quotations in single quotation marks (' ').

> The protagonist slowly comes to recognize that she feels happy about the news of Mr. Mallard's death. She repeats "over and over under her breath: 'free, free, free!'" Obviously, her mood is not, at this point in the story, one of sorrow over her husband's demise.

6. Conventionally, stories are written using the past tense, as in "Once upon a time, there <u>was</u> a young man who <u>set</u> out to seek his fortune." However, when writing about the events that occur in a literary work, you should use the present tense, as in

> In the story a young man <u>leaves</u> home to seek his fortune.

When quoting, you might have to change the tenses of verbs to make them work grammatically in your sentences. Again, any changes that you make within a quotation should be placed in brackets:

> Mrs. Mallard notices that there is a "delicious breath of rain" in the air and that "sparrows [are] twittering in the eaves."

7. Sometimes, you may wish to leave out some of the words within a quotation. Use **ellipsis points** (. . .) to indicate any words that are missing.

> Mrs. Mallard notices "countless sparrows . . . twittering in the eaves."

8. Use a period and ellipsis points (. . . .) when omitting a sentence or more from a quotation, if complete sentences precede and follow the missing information.

> Mrs. Mallard looks forward to her life on her own. The narrator says that "Her fancy was running riot along those days ahead of her. . . . It was only yesterday she had thought with a shudder that life might be long."

9. Always use a comma to set off speaker's tags such as *he says* or *she replies*.

> Josephine asks Mrs. Mallard to open the door. Mrs. Mallard replies, "Go away. I am not making myself ill."

10. A colon may be used to introduce a quotation in a formal way, especially after phrases such as *Here are* or *the following*.

> Mrs. Mallard is truthful when she says the following to her sister: "I am not making myself ill." In fact, Mrs. Mallard is "drinking in a very elixir of life through that open window."

11. Always place periods and commas at the ends of quotations within the quotation marks. Place other punctuation marks, such as colons, semicolons, question marks, and exclamations, outside the quotation marks except when they are part of the quotation.

> Why does Mrs. Mallard tell her sister to "Go away"?

> Josephine asks, "What are you doing, Louise?" and her sister replies, "Go away."

GUM: ("A Birthday," <u>A Birthday</u>) is a great poem!   Using Quotations as Evidence in Your Writing   155

File	Activity	Edit	Help

See Movie
Call Friend
Listen to CDs
Do Activities, Lesson 3.6
Go to Concert
Go Shopping

A. Incorporating Quotations I

Read the following selections. Then rewrite the sentences below, correcting the errors in the punctuation of quotations and paraphrases.

A. By the rude bridge that arched the flood,
  Their flag to April's breeze unfurled,
  Here once the embattled farmers stood,
  And fired the shot heard round the world.

B. "Come back!" the boy called to his friend. Jimmy could not hear him, however. The river was raging, high and wild, and its sound drowned out all else. Jimmy was already halfway across the narrow footbridge, and there was nothing to be done. Mike watched as the bridge collapsed. Minutes later, Jimmy washed up on the bank a hundred yards down, safe but sopping.

1. The boy says "Come back"! but Jimmy cannot hear him.

2. "Jimmy fell into river but did not drown."

3. Concord Bridge crosses over the Concord River near Lexington, Massachusetts. It was "Here once the embattled farmers stood, and fired the shot heard round the world.

4. The setting plays a crucial role in the scene. The river "was raging, and its sound drowned out all else." Because the river is so loud, Jimmy couldn't hear his friend calling.

5. The first stanza is made musical by its rhymes and by alliteration, the repetition of the initial *f* sound in words and phrases like the following "the flood," "their flag," "unfurled," "the farmers," and "fired".

B. Incorporating Quotations 2

Write your own examples to illustrate each rule from the chart on pages 154 and 155.

ANSWER: "A Birthday"

Lesson 3.7

Outlining a Composition to Contrast Literary Works

See Movie
Call Friend
Listen to CDs
Read Lesson 3.7
Go to Concert
Go Shopping

Essays That Contrast

The writing prompt in the Pretest on page 116 asks you to write an essay that contrasts the treatment of death in two literary works. Specifically, the prompt asks you to contrast the attitudes toward death held by the speaker of the poem and the character in the short story. When you **compare** two things, you show how they are **similar.** When you **contrast** two things, you show how they are **different.** The **contrast essay** is an extended piece of writing, several paragraphs long, that describes differences.

Organizing an Essay That Contrasts

A simple way to organize an essay that contrasts is to write five paragraphs. The first paragraph—the introduction—presents the thesis statement. This should be a general statement that describes the subject of the essay (the main difference between the two works) and mentions the titles and authors of the works. For example, a thesis statement for the writing prompt on page 116 might look like this:

Thesis Statement: John Donne's poem "Death, Be Not Proud" and the selection from Leo Tolstoy's short story "The Death of Iván Illych" present very different views of death. In particular, the speaker in Donne's poem has no fear of death, whereas the character Iván Illych fears death exceedingly.

Notice that this thesis statement is two sentences long. It is okay to use two sentences for a thesis statement, as long as the sentences are clear and succinct (not wordy).

Each of the three body paragraphs of the essay may present one difference related to the thesis statement. The topic sentence will state the difference, and the rest of the paragraph will use evidence from the works to back up the topic sentence. Read the outline, on the next page, for a paragraph that relates tone in the two works to the thesis statement.

VOC: Words with prefix *mis–*, meaning "not" or "bad"   Outlining a Composition to Contrast Works   *157*

Rough Outline

Difference in tone in the two works

—Tone of "Death, Be Not Proud"

    —Defiant, scornful toward death

    —Addresses death directly (apostrophe technique), saying that death is not "Mighty and dreadful"

    —Personifies death, accusing death of being proud

        —"be not proud"

        —"why swell'st thou then?"

—Tone of selection from "The Death of Iván Illych"

    —Fearful, disbelieving

    —Illych characterized as in "despair, day and night"

    —Illych filled with "horror and disgust"

    —Illych says, "this cannot be so"

    —Diction (word choice): "despair," "absurd, " "horror," "disgust," "creeping," "ghastly," "terrible," "murderer

Paragraph Based on Outline

First, the different attitudes toward death in the two works are revealed by the differences in tone. The tone of the speaker in "Death, Be Not Proud" is defiant and scornful toward death. The speaker addresses death directly throughout the poem, using the literary technique known as apostrophe. In the first line of the poem, the speaker chastises death, saying, "be not proud." Near the end of the poem, the speaker repeats the chastisement, asking in line 13, "why swell'st thou then?" Clearly, the speaker's tone toward death is one of dismissal. In contrast, the protagonist in the selection from "The Death of Iván Illych" has a fearful, disbelieving attitude. He refuses at first even to think about death, but he cannot keep from doing so. Throughout, the narrator's diction, or word choice, communicates the speaker's disbelief and fearfulness. Such words as "despair," "absurd," "horror," "disgust," "creeping," "ghastly," "terrible," and "murderer" demonstrate this fearful, disbelieving attitude.

The conclusion of the essay can simply restate the thesis and the three main points from the body of the essay using other words.

　ANSWER: misinform, mistaken, misused, misanthrope

File   Activity   Edit   Help

See Movie
Call Friend
Listen to CDs
Do Activities, Lesson 3.7
Go to Concert
Go Shopping

A. Creating an Outline for a Contrast Essay 1

Create a complete rough outline for an essay based on the writing prompt on page 116. You can use the outline for paragraph 2 of the essay from the preceding page. Here are some possible topics for paragraphs 3 and 4 of the essay:

- Difference in personification of death in the two works (in poem, death is a slave and will die; in story, death is an unwelcome guest, a thief, a bill collector, and a murderer, all to be feared)

- Difference in theme of the two works

B. Creating an Outline for a Contrast Essay 2

Another way to organize an essay that contrasts two works is to write four paragraphs—an introduction, a conclusion, and two body paragraphs, each of which deals with one of the works. Look again at Exercise C on page 152. This exercise asked you to think of ways that "A Birthday" and "The Story of an Hour" differ in their portrayals of love. Use the information that you gathered in the comparison-and-contrast chart to create a rough outline for a four-paragraph essay that describes how these two works differ in their portrayal of a character's attitude toward her romantic partner. Your paragraphs should take this form:

- The first paragraph should present the thesis—a statement of how the two selections differ with respect to their portrayals of a romantic relationship

- The second paragraph should deal with one of the selections, explaining what it has to say about love

- The third paragraph should deal with the other selection, explaining what it has to say about love

- The fourth and concluding paragraph should summarize what has been said in the rest of the essay, drawing, again, a sharp contrast between the two selections

In your outline, make sure to refer to specific passages and literary techniques used in the selections.

Lesson 3.8

Taking Part 3 of the Exam: A Summary

See Movie
Call Friend
Listen to CDs
Read Lesson 3.8
Go to Concert
Go Shopping

The following is a complete list of the steps that you must take during Part 3 of the Comprehensive Examination. Follow these steps when you take the Posttest on pages 162–164.

1. Read the writing prompt very carefully. On your scrap paper, make note of

    • The titles and authors of the two pieces you are to read

    • The topic (the aspect of the selections to be contrasted—e.g., treatment of love)

    • Any specific elements of the selections that you are to treat in your essay

2. As you read the selections, keep your topic in mind. Take notes on specific examples and literary techniques related to your subject. Use a rough outline form, in combination with other graphic organizers, if you wish, for your notes.

3. After reading the selections, you will answer some multiple-choice questions about them. As you answer these questions, make use of the strategies described on page 45.

4. Begin your writing process by making a quick rough outline of your composition. Use the five-paragraph or four-paragraph form described in the preceding lesson. The outline for your introduction should include a thesis statement, or controlling idea, that contrasts the two works and mentions the titles and the authors of both works. If you have chosen the four-paragraph form for your essay, then the outline for each of the body paragraphs deals primarily with only one of the two works. It should include a main idea relating the work to the subject of the essay and specific

ANSWER: megalith, megalosaur, megalomania

evidence from the selection, including quotations and literary techniques, that supports your main idea. If you have chosen the five-paragraph form, then the outline for each body paragraph should begin with a main idea that presents one contrasting element (such as a difference in tone or characterization). The outline for each body paragraph should include specific details and literary techniques related to this contrasting element. You do not have to write a rough outline for the conclusion because it will simply restate your thesis and main points in other words.

5. Write the introduction. Make sure that your introductory paragraph mentions the authors and titles of both pieces and that it makes a generalization about how the works differ with respect to the characteristic that is the subject of the essay. Make sure to write neatly. Sloppiness can lower your score!

6. Write the three paragraphs of the body of your composition, using information from your notes. Follow your rough outline. Make sure to mention specific literary techniques in your body paragraphs and to support your statements with quotations from the selection or with paraphrases or summaries of parts of the selection.

7. Finally, write the conclusion. You may wish to begin with a transition such as *In conclusion* or with a question that restates your thesis (e.g., "How do these two selections differ in regard to their treatment of death? First, they . . ."). In your conclusion, restate in other words the main ideas that you presented in the body of the composition.

8. After you have finished writing your composition, read it over carefully. Proofread it for errors in spelling, grammar, usage, punctuation, and capitalization. Make particularly sure that you have used quotation marks correctly throughout. Also make sure that you have punctuated titles correctly. Titles of short works, such as poems, short memoirs, short stories, and so on, should appear in quotation marks. Titles of long works, such as novels or book-length autobiographies, should be underlined (e.g., a selection from <u>The Diary of Anne Frank</u>). Also make particularly certain that names of characters and places are spelled properly and that all proper nouns and adjectives, including character's names, have initial capitals.

Lesson 3.9

Posttest: Part 3

See Movie
Call Friend
Listen to CDs
Take Posttest: Part 3
Go to Concert
Go Shopping

Part 3: Reading and Writing for Literary Response

Directions: Read the poem "A Birthday," on page 130, and "The Story of an Hour," on pages 141–44. Then answer the multiple-choice questions and write a response based on the situation described below. You may use scrap paper to take notes as you read and to plan your written response.

Your Task:

> After you have read the passages and answered the multiple-choice questions, write a unified essay in which you contrast the attitudes toward love held by the speaker of the poem and by the character in the short story. In your essay, use ideas from both passages to develop your thesis. Using evidence from each passage, show how specific literary elements and techniques are used to convey the attitudes expressed in the selections.

Guidelines:

Be sure to

- Discuss the conflicting attitudes toward love revealed in the selections
- Show how specific literary elements (e.g., theme, setting, and characterization) and specific techniques (e.g., symbolism and imagery) help to convey the attitudes expressed in each selection
- Organize your ideas in a unified and coherent manner
- Follow the conventions of standard written English

ANSWER: politics, metropolis, megalopolis

Multiple-Choice Questions

Directions: Use your notes to answer the following questions about the selections. Select the best suggested answer and write its letter on your answer sheet. The questions may help you think of ideas about the selections that you might want to use in your writing. You may return to these questions any time you wish.

1. Both "A Birthday" and "The Story of an Hour" deal with a kind of metaphorical
   (a) death.
   (b) rebirth.
   (c) wealth.
   (d) sadness.

2. The two works make very different symbolic uses of
   (a) an accident.
   (b) trees.
   (c) doves and pomegranates.
   (d) peacocks.

3. The protagonist in "The Story of an Hour" joyfully anticipates
   (a) news that her husband is not dead.
   (b) staying in her room.
   (c) the coming of spring.
   (d) living on her own as a free person.

4. In the fifth paragraph on page 143, Mrs. Mallard thinks to herself, "A kind intention or a cruel intention made the act seem no less a crime as she looked upon it in that brief moment of illumination." What act does she view as a "crime"?
   (a) the killing of her husband
   (b) the attempt by one person to control another
   (c) taking pleasure in the freedom made possible by her husband's death
   (d) her husband's love for her

5. Josephine worries that her sister, Mrs. Mallard, is making herself sick from grief over her husband, but actually, Mrs. Mallard is feeling joy. This is an example of
   (a) understatement.
   (b) irony.
   (c) symbolism.
   (d) metaphor.

6. Images from nature in both works help to create a _____ of joyful anticipation.
   (a) setting
   (b) theme
   (c) mood
   (d) characterization

7. Which word best expresses the feeling of the speaker in "A Birthday" toward the coming of her beloved?
   (a) indifference
   (b) dread
   (c) delight
   (d) distress

8. Which words do not describe images from nature that appear in "A Birthday"?
   (a) happy, festive
   (b) abundant, fruitful
   (c) ominous, gray
   (d) fancy, regal

9. The third paragraph on page 144 says of Mrs. Mallard, "It was only yesterday she had thought with a shudder that life might be long." What was she thinking yesterday?
   (a) that her heart condition would not cut her life short after all
   (b) that her life would seem long because it loomed empty and meaningless
   (c) that the prospect of living with a fatal illness was dreadful
   (d) that life without her husband would be one long, lonely day after another

10. Mrs. Mallard thinks, "What could love, the unsolved mystery, count for in face of this possession of self-assertion which she suddenly recognized as the strongest impulse of her being!" What does this mean?
   (a) Love is a mysterious force but it can be comprehended.
   (b) Love is the driving force of her life.
   (c) Her love is overshadowed by her desire to assert herself.
   (d) Her love is a changing, not a constant, emotion.

ANSWER: hemoglobin, hemophiliac, hemorrhage

Lesson 3.10
Proofreading Workshop

See Movie
Call Friend
Listen to CDs
Read Lesson 3.10
Go to Concert
Go Shopping

Use these proofreading symbols to proofread the paragraphs that follow for errors in spelling, grammar, usage, punctuation, capitalization, and quotation.

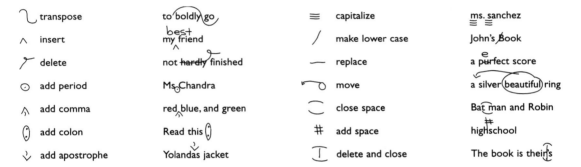

⤿ transpose	to boldly go	≡ capitalize	ms. sanchez
∧ insert	best / my friend	/ make lower case	John's Book
⟋ delete	not hardly finished	— replace	a purfect score (e)
⊙ add period	Ms. Chandra	⌒ move	a silver (beautiful) ring
⩕ add comma	red, blue, and green	⌣ close space	Bat man and Robin
⦂ add colon	Read this	# add space	highschool
⩗ add apostrophe	Yolandas jacket	⊤ delete and close	The book is theirs

The poem Death Be Not Proud, by John Donne and the selection from leo tolstoy's short story "Death of Iván Illych" provides opportuntys for the reader to explore two very diffrent attitudes toward death. The speaker of "Death, Be Not Proud" fearlessly disdains death. Viewing it as a release into eternal life, whereas the main character in "The Death of Iván Illych" fears death. Thinking of it as the end of all his "thoughts and experiences"

First, the tone of the two selections dramatically ilustrates the differences in the two views of death. The speaker in "Death, Be Not Proud" sets the tone for his comments in the first line when he chastises death for being to proud, through out the poem, the speaker takes a haughty tone toward death, expresing the opinion that death has no reason to be prideful because death is actually "a slave" and will itself die. The protagonist in "The Death of Iván Illych," in

GUM: (Hopefully, I hope) I will win a prize.

contrast, has a fearful disbelieving tone. He refuses at first even to think about death. But he can not keep from doing so. The diction, or word choice used throughout the selection communicates the speakers disbelief and fearfulness. Such words as "despair," "absurd," "horror," "disgust," "creeping, ghastly," "terrible," and "murderer" create this fearfull, disbelieving tone

Second both poems personify death, but the personifications in the two works are very different, revealing, again, different attitudes toward the inevitable. In "Death, Be Not Proud," death is personified as being "slave to fate, chance, kings, and desperate men (line 9)" and as something that itself will die. In contrast, death is personified in Tolstoy's story as something truly to be feared, as an "unwelcome guest," as "a highwayman or a thief in a dark alleyway," and as "a bill collector—or worse, a murderer."

Third, the themes, or main ideas, of the selections reveal very different attitudes toward death. The theme of "Death, Be Not Proud" is that death has no real power over people because, as the speaker says in lines 9 and 10, "One short sleep past we wake eternally and death shall be no more." The speaker metaphorically compares death to a short sleep. From which we shall soon awaken. In contrast the main idea of the selection from "The Death of Iván Illych" appears to be that

some people, like Ivan Illych, are intensely afraid of their own death. That they attempt to deny the "simple but somehow absurd concept" that death will come to them. Because there afraid.

ANSWER: I hope

Part 4:

Reading and Writing for Critical Analysis and Evaluation

"Literature makes
comprehensible the myriad
ways in which human beings
meet the infinite possibilities
that life offers."

—Louise Rosenblatt,
Literature as Exploration

Lesson 4.1

Pretest: Part 4

See Movie
Call Friend
Listen to CDs
Take Pretest: Part 4
Go to Concert
Go Shopping

The test booklet for the Comprehensive English Examination looks like the test in this lesson. Take this Pretest as if you were taking the actual exam.

HIGH SCHOOL

COMPREHENSIVE EXAMINATION

IN

ENGLISH

PART 4

This part of the examination tests your ability to interpret a statement and apply it to works of literature. You are to write a critical essay, as directed.

DO NOT TURN THE PAGE UNTIL THE SIGNAL IS GIVEN.

GUM: We (passed, past) our exit!

Part 4: Reading and Writing for Critical Analysis and Evaluation

Your Task:

Write a critical essay in which you discuss **two** works of literature that you have read from the particular perspective of the statement that is provided for you in the **Critical Lens.** In your essay, provide a valid interpretation of the statement, agree **or** disagree with the statement as you have interpreted it, and support your opinion using specific references to appropriate literary elements from the two works. You may use scrap paper to plan your response.

Critical Lens:

> "Literature makes comprehensible the myriad ways in which human beings meet the infinite possibilities that life offers."
>
> —critic Louise Rosenblatt

Guidelines:

Be sure to

- Provide a valid interpretation of the Critical Lens that clearly establishes the criteria for analysis
- State whether you agree or disagree with Rosenblatt's view of what literature does
- Select two works you have read that you believe best support your opinion
- Use the criteria suggested by the Critical Lens to analyze the works you have chosen
- Avoid plot summary. Instead, use specific references to appropriate literary elements (e.g., plot, setting, characterization, tone, theme, figurative language) to show how the works you have chosen support your opinion about the Critical Lens statement
- Organize your ideas in a unified and coherent manner
- Follow the conventions of standard written English
- Specify the titles and authors of the literature you use

ANSWER: passed

Lesson 4.2

Understanding Part 4 of the English Exam

See Movie
Call Friend
Listen to CDs
Read Lesson 4.2
Go to Concert
Go Shopping

What You Must Do for Part 4 of the Exam

As you saw when you took the Pretest, in Part 4 of the New Comprehensive Examination in English you must do the following:

1. read a Critical Lens statement
2. write a position paper in which you
   a. explain what the Critical Lens statement means to you
   b. state whether you agree or disagree with the Critical Lens statement
   c. support your opinion using evidence from two works of literature that you have read previously

Thinking About the Writing Prompt

In the lessons that follow, you will learn more about analyzing a Critical Lens statement, applying the Critical Lens to works of literature, writing a position paper, and presenting evidence in support of an opinion. For now, we will concentrate on understanding the parts of the writing prompt. Before continuing with this lesson, go back and reread the writing prompt on page 170. The writing prompt provides a great deal of information about the essay that you must write, as follows:

- **Sources.** The prompt tells you that there are two sources of information for your essay: 1) a statement, which the prompt calls a "Critical Lens," quoted from the work of a writer or critic and 2) two works of literature that you have read previously. Therefore it is important to read some works of literature in preparation for taking the test. More information on this preparation appears in Lesson 4.4.

GUM: He wrote a letter on (stationary, stationery).

- **Topic.** The prompt tells you that the topic is your position, or opinion, on the Critical Lens statement.

- **Form.** The writing prompt tells you that you will be writing a position paper. A **position paper** is a persuasive essay that presents your **position,** or opinion, on an issue. Notice that the prompt does not tell you precisely how many paragraphs you need to write. Unless you are told in the directions to do otherwise, you will be safe in writing a five-paragraph essay for your position paper.

- **Purpose.** The Your Task portion of the prompt instructs you to write a position paper, which is persuasive in purpose. The Your Task presents three goals that your essay must accomplish to achieve the overall purpose. You must explain the Critical Lens, agree or disagree with the Lens, and support your opinion by referring to two works of literature.

- **Organization.** The writing prompt does not tell you how to organize your essay. In a five-paragraph essay, you might explain the Critical Lens, state your opinion, and introduce the titles and authors of the literary works you have selected in the introduction. Then you might support your opinion with reference to the works of literature in the three body paragraphs. Finally, you might summarize how the evidence supports your opinion in a concluding fifth paragraph.

  The guidelines in the prompt tell you to "organize your ideas in a unified and coherent manner." A piece of writing is **organized** if the order of its ideas makes sense. It is **unified** if all of its ideas are related to its thesis statement or controlling purpose. It is **coherent** if its ideas are connected to one another in ways that show the logical relationships among them. One way to connect ideas logically is to use transitions, such as *first, therefore, furthermore, on the other hand, similarly, more importantly*, and *in conclusion*, to join ideas or group of ideas.

- **Development.** The Your Task section of the writing prompt says that you should develop your essay by using **specific references** to **appropriate literary elements to show how** the literary works you have chosen **support your opinion** about the Critical Lens statement.

ANSWER: stationery

Specific references are details from the works of literature that back up your opinion. Here, *specific* means precise, as opposed to general. A general reference to "The Story of an Hour" might be "The author uses many images relating to time." Specific references pertaining to this idea might be:

The title "The Story of an Hour" emphasizes how dramatically an individual's life can change in a short time.

Now that she is free, Mrs. Mallard prays that life might be long.

"She saw beyond the bitter moment a long procession of years to come that would belong to her absolutely."

Literary elements are terms used to analyze and discuss literature. Examples include *plot* and *symbol*. **Appropriate** elements are those that make your point. The references in the preceding paragraph are examples of how an author uses time as a metaphor to describe the experience of her protagonist. (See Lessons 3.3 through 3.5 for discussions of literary terms.)

To show how literary works **support your opinion,** you will find **evidence,** or information in the literary works that makes your point. Then you will present the evidence as quotations, paraphrases, summaries, and descriptions of literary elements and techniques. (See Lesson 3.6 for details on presenting evidence.)

- **Conventions.** The Guidelines section of the writing prompt tells you to follow the conventions of standard written English. **Conventions** are the proper rules for spelling, grammar, punctuation, and capitalization. (See page 208 for a brief description of what to check for in your essay.)

File   Activity   Edit   Help

See Movie
Call Friend
Listen to CDs
Do Activities, Lesson 4.2
Go to Concert
Go Shopping

 Analyzing Writing Prompts

Study the writing prompt below. Then answer these questions:

1. What are the sources of information for the piece of writing?
2. What is the topic?
3. What form will the piece of writing take?
4. What is the purpose of this piece of writing? What specific goals must the writer try to accomplish?

Writing Prompt:

Your Task: Write a position paper in which you explain what the statement below means to you, agree or disagree with the statement, and support your opinion using two works of literature that you have read previously.

Critical Lens: Ernest Hemingway, the American novelist, said, "All good books are alike in that they are truer than if they had really happened."

Guidelines: In your position paper, be sure to:

- Explain what it means to you for great books to be "truer than if they had really happened"
- State whether you agree or disagree with Hemingway's view
- Select two works that you have read previously that you believe best support your opinion (identify by title and author)
- Use specific references to appropriate literary elements (e.g., plot, setting, tone, theme, characterization, figurative language) to show how the works you have chosen support your opinion about the Critical Lens statement
- Organize your ideas in a unified and coherent manner
- Follow the conventions of standard written English

    ANSWER: capital

B. Choosing Sources

Reread the writing prompt for Exercise A on the previous page. Think about the pieces of literature you have read. Choose two pieces that you think would lend themselves to this writing assignment. Write a paragraph explaining why you chose these particular works.

C. Project

Work with other students in a small group to write a prompt for Part 4 of the examination. Follow the format for prompts shown in this lesson. Base your prompt on quotations about life or literature that you find in books of quotations in the library.

GUM: I ate (tuna soda and chips; tuna, soda, and chips).

Lesson 4.3

Analyzing Critical Lens Statements

File   Activity   Edit   Help

See Movie
Call Friend
Listen to CDs
Read Lesson 4.3
Go to Concert
Go Shopping

Defining the Critical Lens Statement

The writing prompt for Part 4 of the Comprehensive Exam is based on a Critical Lens statement. A *lens* is a transparent substance that focuses light passing through it. *Critical* means "based on sound, careful judgment." When the Comprehensive Exam speaks of a **Critical Lens,** it is referring to a statement through which to examine a work or works of literature, using clear reasoning and sound judgment.

For Part 4 of the exam, you will be given a Critical Lens through which to look at works of literature. You will write a **position paper** in which you explain what the statement means to you, state whether you agree with the statement, and then show how two works of literature that you have read support or disprove the Critical Lens statement.

Understanding the Critical Lens Statement

The first step in writing your position paper is to explain what the Critical Lens statement means to you. It may contain words with which you are not familiar, or it may express a complex idea using simple words. In either case, you need to **analyze** the statement—to break it into its parts and examine them in detail. For example, suppose that you need to interpret the statement by critic Louise Rosenblatt that literature provides "experiences that it would not be either possible or wise to introduce into our own lives" and thus enlarges our "knowledge of the world" and "ability to understand and sympathize with others." You should try to **paraphrase,** or state in your own words, what this means. You might say, "Literature allows us to enter into other worlds and others' lives. It lets us participate (through literary characters) in experiences that we could not have ourselves. By so doing, we are able to stretch our idea of the world and to see life through the eyes of others. We understand better how they think, and we learn to feel what they feel."

ANSWER: tuna, soda, and chips

If a Critical Lens statement contains a word you do not know, don't panic. In one of her poems, Emily Dickinson wrote, "There is no frigate like a book / To take us lands away." If you were given this statement as a Critical Lens and did not know the meaning of *frigate*, you could still figure out the meaning of the statement and write a good essay. The second part of the quote indicates that a frigate takes us lands away, so you might guess that a frigate is some means of transportation. (It is a ship.) In your essay, you could focus on how good books transport us to different lands, either real or imaginary.

Suppose you encountered this statement by Henry David Thoreau as a Critical Lens: "The mass of men lead lives of quiet desperation." At first glance, you might not be able to make sense of this statement. If, however, you gave it some careful thought, you would be able to understand it. "The mass of men" is not a common expression, but you might conclude that it means "the majority of people" or "people in general." You might not know what Thoreau means by "quiet desperation," but you probably know the related word *desperate*, which means "feeling hopeless" or "driven to extremes by despair." You could guess that "quiet desperation" means an inner sense of hopelessness. You could conclude that Thoreau is saying that most people go through life with an inner sense of hopelessness. In your essay you could explain how this statement is supported or disproved by two literary works.

Formulating a Thesis Statement

Once you have explained the meaning of the Critical Lens, you need to state whether you agree with it. Think about your interpretation. Ask yourself which literary works that you have read will best support your opinion. Then formulate your **thesis statement,** in which you express the opinion that you will defend in your essay. For the quote from Emily Dickinson, you might say, "The poet Emily Dickinson has captured a truth about literature—that it allows the reader to be transported in his or her mind to different times and different places, even into imaginary lands or into the mind of another person." In response to the quote from Thoreau, you could write, "I disagree that most people lead lives of 'quiet desperation'; there are certainly some people who have a clear sense of purpose and a genuine joy in living. James Herriot expresses this in *All Things Bright and Beautiful* and Franklin does in *The Autobiography of Benjamin Franklin*."

GUM: I (got, gots) a B in math.

Sample Critical Lens Statements

The following are some general statements from famous writers and critics. Read these statements. Decide whether you agree or disagree with them and why. Then relate them to two or three full-length works that you have read previously.

1. According to the poet and critic Randall Jarrell, a first-rate work of literature "makes the reader feel that he [or she] is not in a book but in a world, and a world that has in common with [his or her] own some of the things that are most important in both."

2. American essayist Logan Pearsall Smith said, "What I like in a good author is not what he says but what he whispers."

3. The Roman philosopher and statesman Seneca said, "The bravest sight in the world is to see a great man struggling against adversity."

4. The Victorian poet and critic Matthew Arnold said that literature is "at bottom a criticism of life."

5. Swiss psychiatrist Carl Jung stated, "Man needs difficulties; they are necessary for health."

6. John Keats said of poetry, but the same could be said of much of literature, that it "strikes[s] the reader as a wording of his [or her] own highest thoughts and appear[s] almost a remembrance."

7. American humorist Robert Benchley stated, "Great literature must spring from an upheaval in the author's soul. If that upheaval is not present, then it must come from the works of any other author which happens to be handy and easily adapted."

8. According to the critic Northrup Frye, the purpose of literature is to "educate the imagination," to train us to see "what is possible."

9. According to the poet and playwright Oscar Wilde, "It is the spectator [or the reader], and not life, that art really mirrors."

10. What Shakespeare's Hamlet tells the actors about drama can be said, as well, of all literature, that its purpose is "to hold . . . the mirror up to nature" and "to show . . . the very age and body of the time [his] form and pressure."

ANSWER: got

| File | Activity | Edit | Help |

See Movie
Call Friend
Listen to CDs
Do Activities, Lesson 4.3
Go to Concert
Go Shopping

Interpreting Critical Lens Statements

Read the Critical Lens statements below. For each one, give your own interpretation of what the statement means.

Critical Lens 1:

What George Bernard Shaw said of an artist can be said of an author as well: "The artist's work is to show us ourselves as we really are."

Critical Lens 2:

British author Arthur Koestler said, "In the true novel . . . the main action takes place inside the characters' skulls and ribs."

Critical Lens 3:

The English author Rudyard Kipling asserted that "Fiction is Truth's elder sister."

Writing a Thesis Statement

For each Critical Lens statement given below, decide whether you agree or disagree with the statement. Then write a thesis statement for an essay supporting or refuting the statement.

Critical Lens 1:

American author Thornton Wilder observed, "When you're safe at home you wish you were having an adventure; when you're having an adventure you wish you were safe at home."

Critical Lens 2:

The poet T. S. Eliot wrote that literature is "not an assertion of truth, but the making of the truth more fully real to us."

Critical Lens 3:

English statesman Benjamin Disraeli made this provocative comment about books: "Books are fatal: they are the curse of the human race. Nine-tenths of existing books are nonsense, and clever books are the refutation of that nonsense. The greatest misfortune that ever befell (humanity) was the invention of the printing press."

| VOC: Words with prefix *a*, meaning not | Analyzing Critical Lens Statements 179 |

Lesson 4.4
Prior Preparation for Part 4 of the Exam

File   Activity   Edit   Help

See Movie
Call Friend
Listen to CDs
Read Lesson 4.4
Go to Concert
Go Shopping

Preparing for Part 4 of the Exam

In Part 4 of the exam you will be asked to support your opinion about a Critical Lens by referring to two works of literature that you have previously read. These works may be literature that you have read in school or on your own. To do well on this part of the test, it makes sense to prepare in advance. You can do so by studying three works of literature in the time before the test.

To prepare for Part 4 of the exam, make sure that you do the following:

1. Read at least **three** full-length works of literature. The exam prompt asks you to write about only two works, but if you read three, then you will be able to choose the two that are best for your essay. Possible works include short novels, autobiographies, biographies, and plays. Make sure that the works you choose are high-quality literary works. It would be best if you chose two works that you have studied in English class and that you understand thoroughly. Also, make sure that the works you choose are appropriate for students at your grade level. When grading your exam, the examiner might react unfavorably if you have written about pulp fiction, such as popular romance novels, or about works appropriate for young children.

2. Study the three works carefully. Make sure that you can identify the following parts of each work:

    —The **author** and the **title** of the work. The examiner will check to make sure that the author and title are correct. Make sure that you can write these out from memory, spelling them correctly.

    —The **genre,** or type, of the work (i.e., short story, memoir, epic poem, tragedy). See the list of genres on pages 126 and 127.

    —The **theme,** or main idea that the work communicates or teaches.

ANSWER: atypical, atonal, amoral

—If the work is a narrative, the **plot,** including the central conflict, the inciting incident, the rising action, the turning point, the climax, the falling action, and the resolution. (See the description of the parts of a narrative on page 145.)

—The **setting** and **mood** of the work. (See the description of the parts of a narrative on page 145.)

—The **protagonist,** or main character, in the work. Make sure that you can tell what conflict, or struggle, the protagonist faces, what he or she does in response to this conflict, what he or she learns in the course of the work, and how he or she changes.

—Several **literary techniques** used in the work that are related to the work's theme. (See the list of literary techniques on pages 128–31.)

3. Make thorough notes on all the elements and techniques listed above for each of the three works. **This step is extremely important!** The act of making these notes will help you to understand the works and to remember the elements and techniques employed in them. Making notes will also enable you to review just before the exam so that the three works will be fresh in your mind.

4. Choose two short quotations from each work that illustrate the work's major theme, or main idea, and **commit these quotations to memory.** Make sure that you can write them down word for word without looking at the sources. Using one or two of these direct quotations in your essay will help you to make your point strongly.

5. After you have studied the three works, practice writing about them. Write about questions like the following:

   a. In what way does the main character change or grow in the course of the work?

   b. What is the primary or most important message that the work teaches?

   c. With what major conflict does the work deal? How is this conflict introduced, developed, and resolved?

Ideally, before taking the exam, you will study and write about the three works until you know them inside out, backward and forward, from every angle. Then you will be ready for most anything you will encounter in Part 4 of the Comprehensive Examination.

GUM: The (principal, principle) spoke to the assembly.

Choosing Works to Study for the Exam

The following is a partial list of works that would be appropriate for you to read and study in preparation for the exam.

Achebe, *Things Fall Apart*
Aeschylus, *Prometheus Bound*
Allende, *The House of the Spirits*
Anderson, *Winesburg, Ohio*
Angelou, *I Know Why the Caged Bird Sings*
Anon., *Beowulf*
Anon., *Everyman*
Anon., *Ramayana* (retold by Wm. Buck)
Anon., *Sir Gawain and the Green Knight*
Anon., *The Thousand and One Nights*
Austen, *Emma*
——, *Pride and Prejudice*
Baldwin, *The Fire Next Time*
Beckett, *Waiting for Godot*
Bellow, *Henderson the Rain King*
Bolt, *A Man for All Seasons*
Bradbury, *Fahrenheit 451*
Brontë, C., *Jane Eyre*
Brontë, E., *Wuthering Heights*
Brown, *Manchild in the Promised Land*
Byron, *Don Juan*
Cæsar, *The Conquest of Gaul*
Camus, *The Stranger*
Cather, *My Antonia*
Cervantes, *Don Quixote*
Chaucer, *The Canterbury Tales*
Chekhov, *Three Sisters*
Chopin, *The Awakening*
Cisneros, *The House on Mango Street*
Conrad, *Heart of Darkness*
Crane, *The Red Badge of Courage*
Dante, *The Inferno*
Defoe, *Robinson Crusoe*
Dickens, any work
Dillard, *An American Childhood*
Dinesen, *Out of Africa*
Dostoevsky, *Crime and Punishment*
Douglass, *Narrative of the Life of Frederick Douglass*

Dreiser, *Sister Carrie*
Dumas, *The Three Musketeers*
Eliot, G., *Silas Marner*
Eliot, T. S., *Murder in the Cathedral*
Ellison, *Invisible Man*
Euripides, *Medea*
Faulkner, *As I Lay Dying*
——, *The Sound and the Fury*
Filipovic, *A Child's Life in Sarajevo*
Fitzgerald, *The Great Gatsby*
——, *Tender Is the Night*
Flaubert, *Madame Bovary*
Forster, *Howard's End*
——, *A Passage to India*
Frank, *The Diary of a Young Girl*
Fugard, *Master Harold . . . and the Boys*
Galarza, *Barrio Boy*
Goethe, *Faust*
Golding, *Lord of the Flies*
Greene, *The Power and the Glory*
Hansberry, *A Raisin in the Sun*
Hardy, any work
Hawthorne, *The Scarlet Letter*
Hemingway, *A Farewell to Arms*
——, *The Old Man and the Sea*
——, *The Sun Also Rises*
Herriot, *All Creatures Great and Small*
Hesse, *Siddhartha*
Homer, *The Iliad*
——, *The Odyssey*
Hugo, *Les Misérables*
Hurston, *Their Eyes Were Watching God*
Huxley, *Brave New World*
Ibsen, *A Doll's House*
——, *Hedda Gabler*
James, *Daisy Miller*
——, *The Portrait of a Lady*
——, *The Turn of the Screw*
Joyce, *A Portrait of the Artist as a Young Man*

Kafka, *The Metamorphosis*
Kawabata, *The Sound of the Mountain*
Kennedy, *Profiles in Courage*
Keyes, *Flowers for Algernon (Charly)*
Kingston, *The Woman Warrior*
Knowles, *A Separate Peace*
Kosinski, *Being There*
Lawrence, *Sons and Lovers*
Lawrence/Lee, *Inherit the Wind*
Lee, *To Kill a Mockingbird*
Le Guin, *The Dispossessed*
Lewis, *Babbitt*
London, *The Call of the Wild*
Malory, *Le Morte d'Arthur*
Marlowe, *The Tragical History of Dr. Faustus*
Márquez, *One Hundred Years of Solitude*
Masters, *Spoon River Anthology*
Mathabane, *Kaffir Boy*
McCullers, *The Heart Is a Lonely Hunter*
Miller, *The Crucible*
——, *Death of a Salesman*
Milton, *Paradise Lost*
Morrison, *Song of Solomon*
Murasaki, *The Tale of Genji*
Neihardt, *Black Elk Speaks*
O'Neill, *Long Day's Journey into Night*
——, *The Iceman Cometh*
Orwell, *Animal Farm*
——, *1984*
Ovid, *Metamorphoses*
Potok, *The Chosen*
Rodriguez, *Hunger of Memory*
Rose, *Twelve Angry Men*
Rostand, *Cyrano de Bergerac*
Rousseau, *The Confessions*
Salinger, *The Catcher in the Rye*
Santiago, *When I Was Puerto Rican*
Shakespeare, any play
Shaw, *Pygmalion*
——, *Saint Joan*

Shelley, *Frankenstein*
Smith, *A Tree Grows in Brooklyn*
Sophocles, *Antigone*
——, *Oedipus the King*
Steinbeck, *The Grapes of Wrath*
——, *Of Mice and Men*
Stoker, *Dracula*
Sturluson, *The Prose Edda*
Swift, *Gulliver's Travels*
Tan, *The Joy Luck Club*
Thomas, *Under Milkwood*
Thoreau, *Walden*
Tolkein, *The Hobbit*
Tolstoy, *Anna Karenina*
——, *War and Peace*
Townsend, *The Diary of Adrian Mole*
Twain, *Adventures of Huckleberry Finn*
——, *The Adventures of Tom Sawyer*
Verne, *20,000 Leagues Under the Sea*
Virgil, *The Aeneid*
Voltaire, *Candide*
Vonnegut, *Slaughterhouse Five*
Walker, *The Color Purple*
Warren, *All the King's Men*
Wells, *The Invisible Man*
——, *The War of the Worlds*
Wharton, *Ethan Frome*
——, *The Age of Innocence*
White, *The Once and Future King*
Wiesel, *Night*
Wilde, *The Importance of Being Earnest*
Wilder, *Our Town*
Williams, *The Glass Menagerie*
——, *A Streetcar Named Desire*
Wilson, *Fences*
Woolf, *A Room of One's Own*
Wright, *Black Boy*
——, *Native Son*
Yates, *Amos Fortune, Free Man*
Zola, *Germinal*

ANSWER: principal

File   Activity   Edit   Help

See Movie
Call Friend
Listen to CDs
Do Activities, Lesson 4.4
Go to Concert
Go Shopping

A. Examining Elements of a Literary Work

Choose three literary works that you have studied in class. For each work, answer the following questions on your own paper. Use complete sentences.

1. Who is the author of the work? What is the title?
2. What is the genre of the work?
3. What is the theme, or main idea, of the work? (You may, if you wish, identify more than one theme.)
4. Is the work a narrative? With what central conflict does the work deal? If it is a narrative, what is the inciting incident? What happens during the rising action? What is the turning point? What is the climax? What happens during the falling action? How is the central conflict resolved?
5. Who is the protagonist or main character? What conflict does this character face? Is the conflict internal or external? What does this character learn, and how does he or she change in the course of the work?
6. What is the setting of the work? What is its mood?

B. Examining Techniques in a Literary Work

Using the three literary works that you have chosen, find examples of as many literary techniques as you can in the chart on pages 128–130.

C. Reading Literature

Choose three works from the list on page 182, or three other works of comparable quality, and start reading. Make sure to choose works you are going to enjoy, because in order to prepare well for Part 4 of the exam, you are going to have to spend considerable time with these works in the near future.

| GUM: Cæsar (led, lead) the troops into battle. | Prior Preparation for Part 4 of the Exam   *183* |

Lesson 4.5

Writing Your Essay for Part 4 of the Exam

See Movie
Call Friend
Listen to CDs
Read Lesson 4.5
Go to Concert
Go Shopping

Follow the steps enumerated below to write your essay for Part 4 of the exam. See Lessons 1.7 through 1.9 in this book for detailed instruction on writing an essay.

1. Read the exam prompt carefully. Make sure that you understand the Critical Lens statement.

2. Make a brief rough outline of your paper.

3. Write the introduction. The introduction should contain the following parts:

    —Begin with a sentence that contains the Critical Lens, like this one:

    According to Louise Rosenblatt, "literature makes comprehensible the myriad ways in which human beings meet the infinite possibilities that life offers."

    —Next, restate the Critical Lens in your own words:

    In other words, by reading works of literature, we can learn about the many different ways in which people live their lives and about how people choose from among the possibilities that life offers.

    —Finally, state whether you agree or disagree with the Critical Lens, and relate it to the works of literature you have prepared.

    The novel <u>The Grapes of Wrath</u>, by John Steinbeck, and the autobiography <u>My Left Foot</u>, by Christie Brown, both illustrate the truth of Ms. Rosenblatt's statement.

4. Write one body paragraph about each literary work, showing how the work proves or disproves the Critical Lens.

    —Begin with a topic sentence that relates one of the works to the Critical Lens.

    John Steinbeck's novel <u>The Grapes of Wrath</u> shows how the protagonist, Tom Joad, responds to the limitations and possibilities thrust upon him by the Oklahoma Dust Bowl disaster of the 1930s.

ANSWER: led

—Then support your topic sentence with specific evidence from the literary work, making sure to use terms that describe literary elements and techniques.

> The reader of Steinbeck's novel may never have experienced extreme poverty and hardship, but the novel vividly illustrates this way of life. The book details how the Joad family, through no fault of its own, is forced from its home in Oklahoma. The reader follows as the family moves to California to find work, suffering many indignities as migrant laborers, facing hunger, and encountering a system in which wealthy landowners profit from the misery of poverty-stricken workers. Many people would be crushed by the terrible events that the Joads encounter, but one theme of <u>The Grapes of Wrath</u> is that disaster can bring out the best in people. At the beginning of the novel, the protagonist, Tom Joad, has no interest in anything political. In the course of the novel, however, he changes. Instead of crumbling, he seizes the possibility of becoming a labor organizer and working to better the lives of migrants. Life offers Tom Joad a number of possibilities. He chooses not to crumble but to fight back. Tom Joad's response illustrates Steinbeck's central theme that oppressed people will rise against their oppressors. As Tom Joad says at the climax of the novel, "I'll be all aroun' in the dark. I'll be ever'where—wherever you look. Wherever they's a fight so hungry people can eat, I'll be there."

5. In the next paragraph, refer to the second work. Again, use a topic sentence that relates this work to the Critical Lens. Connect the ideas in the body paragraphs with transitions.

> <u>My Left Foot</u>, by Christie Brown, also demonstrates how an individual rises to the occasion when faced with difficult circumstances. In this case, . . .

6. Write a third body paragraph in which you compare both works.

> Brown uses autobiography and Steinbeck fiction, but both authors allow us to see how individuals react with courage to harsh fate.

7. Write the conclusion. The conclusion should restate your position with regard to the Critical Lens and summarize the main points you have made in support of your position.

8. After you have finished your writing, proofread carefully. Be particularly careful to capitalize proper nouns and punctuate correctly.

GUM: Manuel (arrives, arrived) here yesterday.

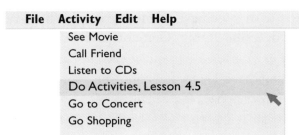

File   Activity   Edit   Help

See Movie
Call Friend
Listen to CDs
Do Activities, Lesson 4.5
Go to Concert
Go Shopping

A. Organizing Information for a Position Paper

Choose one of the Critical Lens statements from page 178 and create a rough outline for a position paper based on the statement. Make sure that your writing plan covers the guidelines given below.

Your Task: Write a position paper in which you explain what the Critical Lens statement means to you, agree or disagree with the statement, and support your opinion using two works from the literature you have studied.

Critical Lens: Choose one statement from the list on page 178.

Guidelines: In your position paper, be sure to

- Explain what the Critical Lens statement means to you
- State whether you agree or disagree with the statement
- Select two works you have studied that you believe best support your opinion
- Use specific references to appropriate literary elements to show how the works you have chosen support your opinion about the Critical Lens statement
- Organize your ideas in a unified and coherent manner
- Follow the conventions of standard written English
- Identify the titles and authors of the literature you use

B. Writing Your Position Paper

Now develop your rough outline into a full, five-paragraph essay. Be sure to use transitions to connect ideas in your essay.

ANSWER: arrived

Lesson 4.6

Taking Part 4 of the Exam: A Summary

See Movie
Call Friend
Listen to CDs
Read Lesson 4.6
Go to Concert
Go Shopping

The following is a complete list of the steps that you must take to prepare for and succeed on Part 4 of the Comprehensive Examination.

A. Before the Exam
    1. Read three works of literature and take notes on them. Make sure that for each work you can identify the title, the author, the genre, the theme, the protagonist or speaker, the plot, the setting, the mood, and any significant literary techniques and elements.
    2. Memorize two short, theme-related quotations from each work so that you can write them word for word.
    3. Practice writing about the three works.

B. During the Exam
    1. Read the prompt. Paraphrase the Critical Lens to help you understand it.
    2. Make a brief rough outline of your essay.
    3. Write your introduction. Include:
        • A restatement of the Critical Lens
        • An explanation of what the Critical Lens means to you
        • A statement agreeing or disagreeing with the Critical Lens
        • A thesis statement that indicates that your position on the Critical Lens can be supported by two works of literature
        • The titles and authors of the two works of literature
        • (Note that the last three items can be combined in a single statement. See the example on page 184.)
    4. Write body paragraphs in which you support your position using specific evidence from both works of literature.
    5. Write a conclusion in which you restate your position regarding the Critical Lens and summarize the main points made in your essay.

Lesson 4.7

Posttest: Part 4

See Movie
Call Friend
Listen to CDs
Take Posttest: Part 4
Go to Concert
Go Shopping

Part 4: Reading and Writing for Critical Analysis and Evaluation

Your Task:

Write a critical essay in which you discuss **two** works of literature that you have read from the particular perspective of the statement that is provided for you in the **Critical Lens.** In your essay, provide a valid interpretation of the statement, agree **or** disagree with the statement as you have interpreted it, and support your opinion using specific references to appropriate literary elements from the two works. You may use scrap paper to plan your response.

Critical Lens:

> "Every work of literature leads up to one great moment of insight, one instant in which truth stands revealed."   —poet Teresa Melos

Guidelines:

Be sure to

- Provide a valid interpretation of the Critical Lens that clearly establishes the criteria for analysis
- State whether you agree or disagree with Melos's view of what literature does
- Select two works that you have read that you believe best support your opinion
- Use the criteria suggested by the Critical Lens to analyze the works
- Avoid plot summary. Instead, use specific references to appropriate literary elements (e.g., plot, setting, characterization, tone, theme, figurative language) to show how the works you have chosen support your opinion about the Critical Lens statement
- Organize your ideas in a unified and coherent manner
- Follow the conventions of standard written English
- Specify the titles and authors of the literature you use

     ANSWER: betrayal, reversal, vocal

Part 5:

Complete Practice Test

"Self-confidence is the first
requisite to great undertakings."

—Dr. Samuel Johnson

190

Complete Practice Test: Session 1

The test booklet for the Comprehensive English Examination will look similar to what you find in this lesson. The first two parts are given in one session. Take this Practice Test as if you were taking the real exam.

HIGH SCHOOL

COMPREHENSIVE EXAMINATION

IN

ENGLISH

SESSION 1

This session of the examination has two parts. The first part tests listening skills; you are to listen as a selection is read aloud, answer the multiple-choice questions, and write a response, as directed. For the second part, you will read informational material, answer multiple-choice questions, and write a response, as directed. On page 207 of this book, you will find a sample answer sheet for the multiple-choice questions. To take the test in this book, you will use your own paper to answer the multiple-choice questions and write your essay.

DO NOT TURN THE PAGE UNTIL THE SIGNAL IS GIVEN.

Part 1: Listening and Writing for Information and Understanding

Overview: For this part of the test, you will listen to a lecture about the volcanic eruption that destroyed the ancient Roman city of Pompeii. Then you will write a response based on the situation described below. You will also answer some multiple-choice questions about key ideas in the lecture. You will hear the lecture twice. You may take notes on a separate piece of paper at any time you wish during the readings.

> **The Situation:** You have a summer job working for a travel company that takes groups of high-school students to sites of historical and educational interest in Europe. Your supervisor, the owner of the travel company, has asked you to attend a lecture about the eruption at Pompeii. You are supposed to use information from the lecture to write a short, informative pamphlet providing background information to students who will be visiting Pompeii in a few weeks. In preparation for writing your pamphlet, listen to the lecture given by writer Robin Shulka. Then use relevant information from the lecture to write your pamphlet.

Your Task: Write a pamphlet to be given to high-school students to provide them with background information on Pompeii.

Guidelines:

Be sure to

- Explain to your audience what happened in Pompeii almost two thousand years ago
- Explain why Pompeii is of interest to modern archaeologists and might be of interest to the students
- Use accurate, specific information from the lecture
- Organize your ideas in a unified and coherent manner
- Follow the conventions of standard written English

Multiple-Choice Questions

Directions: Use your notes to answer the following questions about the lecture. Select the best answer and write its letter on your answer sheet. The questions may help you think of ideas from the lecture to use in your writing. You may return to these questions any time you wish

1. **Viewing the ruins of Pompeii gives a modern visitor an opportunity to see what life was like in an ancient**
   (a) Roman city.
   (b) Italian villa.
   (c) Chinese village.
   (d) feudal state.

2. **The destruction of Pompeii occurred in**
   (a) 63 B.C.
   (b) 79 B.C.
   (c) A.D. 63.
   (d) A.D. 79.

3. **The article mentions plaster casts made of**
   (a) buildings from Pompeii.
   (b) bread, figs, olives, and other foodstuffs from Pompeii.
   (c) the bodies of people and animals who died at Pompeii.
   (d) all of the above.

4. **A modern visitor to Pompeii can see ancient Roman**
   (a) homes.
   (b) shops.
   (c) public facilities.
   (d) homes, shops, and public facilities.

5. **The speaker likens visiting Pompeii to**
   (a) going to the moon.
   (b) traveling in an exotic country.
   (c) taking a trip in a time machine.
   (d) reading a book.

6. **Pompeii was**
   (a) buried under ashes and later dug up in a well-preserved condition.
   (b) sunk beneath the ocean and later raised up in a well-preserved condition.
   (c) leveled by an earthquake but later pieced together by archaeologists.
   (d) destroyed by a fire and later rebuilt.

7. **The destruction of Pompeii occurred**
   (a) about two hundred years ago.
   (b) almost two thousand years ago.
   (c) about two decades ago.
   (d) over five thousand years ago.

8. **Among the ancient artworks that a modern visitor can see at Pompeii, the article mentions**
   (a) mosaics.
   (b) frescoes.
   (c) statues.
   (d) all of the above.

Part 2: Reading and Writing for Information and Understanding

Directions: Read the magazine article on the following pages, answer the multiple-choice questions, and write a response based on the situation described below. You may use scrap paper to take notes as you read and to plan your written response.

> **The Situation:** You have been asked to write a column for your school newspaper about guidelines for staying healthy and fit. The article is supposed to provide suggestions for healthy eating and exercise. To prepare for writing your article, you contact a nutritional sports medicine consultant, Anita Shriver, who sends you a copy of her magazine article, "Old Saying, New Meaning: Everything in Moderation." Read the magazine article carefully and take notes on it.

Your Task: Using relevant information from the article and the accompanying graphic material, write a column for your school newspaper on exercising and eating well to stay fit.

Guidelines:

Be sure to

- Suggest guidelines for exercising
- Suggest guidelines for healthy eating
- Use accurate, specific information from the magazine article and from the accompanying visual materials
- Use a tone and voice appropriate for a column in a student newspaper
- Organize your ideas in a unified and coherent manner
- Follow the conventions of standard written English

Old Saying, New Meaning: Everything in Moderation
by Anita Shriver

Glance at some of the popular magazines sold at your local supermarket checkout counter, and you'll see that Americans are obsessed with dieting and fitness. Every week, as I stand waiting for the cashier to ring through my low-fat sorbet, mineral water, and celery sticks, those magazine covers stare back at me, announcing articles with titles like "Ten Days to a New You," "Better Abs for a Better Life," "Use It and Lose It," and "The Do-or-Die Diet." Usually, there is at least one book on dieting or fitness on the *New York Times* nonfiction bestseller list, and the health and fitness sections of bookstores are among the largest. You would think, given all the ink spilled on these subjects, that Americans would be the healthiest people on Earth and the most knowledgeable about nutrition and exercise. If you were to think that, you would be wrong. The problem is that much of what is written about diet and exercise is produced to sell products—weight machines, food supplements, weight-loss plans, and the like—and there's a lot of misinformation out there.

The Dangers of Dieting and Fitness Fads

All the books and magazines published in America on these subjects reflect a national concern: Many Americans feel that they are not eating right, that they are not in good condition, that they are overweight, and so on. Worry about these matters makes us easy prey for the latest exercise or dieting fads. Unfortunately, these fads can be dangerous. For example, in recent years, a low-carbohydrate[1] diet has been widely promoted for weight loss, but such a diet can raise cholesterol[2] levels and make the dieter less healthy. Another fad that has swept the United States in recent years is intense athletic activity—hours of grueling mountain biking, rock climbing, jogging, and other vigorous, calorie-burning activities. However, for people who are not in good shape, such activities can actually be dangerous, leading, for example, to heart attacks.

---

[1] **carbohydrate.** Any of a number of organic compounds contained in food, including sugars, starches, and celluloses

[2] **cholesterol.** A substance found in animal products, such as meat and milk, that, if consumed in excess, can cause plaque build-up in blood vessels and lead to heart attacks and strokes

The Value of Moderation

The point is that in regard to both diet and exercise, scientific evidence supports the conclusion that your grandmother's old saying, "everything in moderation," is the best advice. That's the recommendation of a new report, jointly published by the Department of Agriculture (USDA) and the Department of Health and Human Services (HHS), called *Nutrition and Your Health: Dietary Guidelines for Americans.* Let's consider exercise and nutrition in turn.

Sensible Exercising. Exercise is good for you, don't get me wrong; however, it is important to exercise sensibly. Before beginning any strenuous exercise routine, make sure to get a physical checkup to ensure that you're up to it. Start slowly, and build up your stamina over time. Then, keep your exercise routine within reasonable limits. The USDA and HHS recommend *30 minutes of vigorous, high-intensity activity at least three times a week* to promote cardiovascular[3] fitness. However, for the rest of the week, and this is the big news, the recommendation is for *moderate activity daily.* In other words, extreme, grueling daily workouts are not necessary. As a 1995 Mayo Clinic Health Letter

---

[3] **cardiovascular.** Having to do with the heart and the blood vessels as a unified bodily system (the circulatory system)

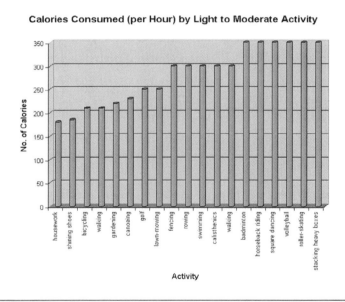

Calories Consumed (per Hour) by Light to Moderate Activity

A **calorie** is a unit used to measure the energy produced by food when it is used by the body. Of course, not all food is converted to energy. Some is turned into waste products, and some is made into bodily tissues. If a person consumes many more calories than he or she needs for energy or for normal bodily maintenance and growth, then the excess will be stored in the body as fat. As the chart shows, even moderate activities can burn lots of calories and keep a person trim.

suggests: "It's time to exercise. So get out and mow the lawn. Or play a game of badminton. Or, better yet, call a friend and hit the links." As the chart on the previous page shows, moderate physical activity, such as taking a brisk walk, gardening, doing calisthenics, or even doing housework, can burn calories. Daily moderate activity can also go a long way, the USDA and HHS suggest, toward keeping you healthy.

Sensible Eating. With regard to diet, moderation is also in order. The USDA/HHS report suggests that people should eat a wide variety of foods, including lots of fruits, vegetables, and grains, and maintain a diet low in fat, saturated fat, and cholesterol. For adults, *no more than 30 percent of daily calories, averaged over several days, should come from fat.* Crash diets and rapid weight loss should be avoided, as these can be extremely stressful on the system, and diet plans should be undertaken only on the advice and under the monitoring of a physician. A good guideline for eating well is the **USDA Food Pyramid,** which suggests eating *lots of bread, cereal, rice, pasta, vegetables, and fruit and adding two or three servings of dairy products and two or three servings of meat products.*

All of this just goes to show you that your grandmother's advice wasn't so bad after all. "Everything in moderation"—remember that phrase and forget the fads from the books and articles.

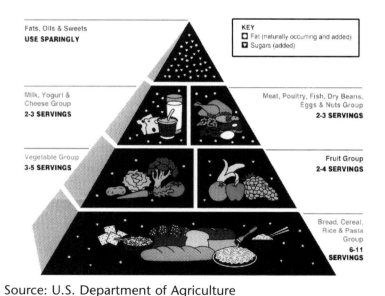

Source: U.S. Department of Agriculture

The **Food Pyramid** was created by the USDA as a guide to sensible, moderate eating. As the pyramid suggests, a person's diet should contain large amounts of bread, cereal, rice, and pasta; smaller amounts of vegetables and fruits; still smaller amounts of dairy products, meats, beans, and eggs; and very small amounts of fats, oils, and sweets.

Multiple-Choice Questions

Directions: Select the best suggested answer to each question and write its letter on your answer sheet. The questions may help you think about ideas and information that you might want to use in your writing. You may return to these questions any time you wish.

1. According to Anita Shriver, Americans feel that they are not eating right, that they are not in good condition, and that they are overweight. As a result, they are "easy prey" for
   (a) nutritional advice from the USDA.
   (b) nutritional advice from the HHS.
   (c) exercise and dieting fads.
   (d) people who sell cookbooks.

2. The main idea of Ms. Shriver's article is that exercise and eating should be
   (a) enjoyable.
   (b) done in moderation.
   (c) done in the early morning.
   (d) intense and vigorous.

3. The word *moderate* means
   (a) excessive, extreme, or intense.
   (b) with great frequency.
   (c) kept within reasonable limits, not overdone.
   (d) done occasionally or not at all.

4. Examples of moderate exercise mentioned by Ms. Shriver are
   (a) mountain biking and skiing.
   (b) jogging and rock climbing.
   (c) tennis and wrestling.
   (d) brisk walking and gardening.

5. According to the USDA/HHS report, moderate physical exercise should be done for 30 minutes
   (a) once a week.
   (b) twice a week.
   (c) three times a week.
   (d) daily.

6. According to the USDA/HHS report, no more than 30% of daily calories, averaged over several days, should come from
   (a) milk.
   (b) cheese.
   (c) fat.
   (d) meat.

7. According to the graph, gardening for one hour consumes about
   (a) 150 calories.
   (b) 180 calories.
   (c) 200 calories.
   (d) 350 calories.

8. According to the food pyramid, daily food consumption should include approximately ___ servings of bread, cereal, rice, and pasta.
   (a) 2–3
   (b) 2–4
   (c) 3–5
   (d) 6–11

HIGH SCHOOL

COMPREHENSIVE EXAMINATION

IN

ENGLISH

SESSION 2

This session of the examination has two parts. For the first part, you are to answer ten multiple-choice questions and write a response, as directed. For the second part, you will interpret a statement and write a response, as directed. On page 207 of this book, you will find a sample answer sheet for the multiple-choice questions. To take the test in this book, you will use your own paper to answer the multiple-choice questions and write your essay.

DO NOT TURN THE PAGE UNTIL THE SIGNAL IS GIVEN.

Part 3: Reading and Writing for Literary Response

Directions: Read the poem "Boast Not, Proud English," by Roger Williams, and a selection from "Remarks Concerning the Natives of North America," an essay by Benjamin Franklin. Write the letter of the answer to each multiple-choice question on your answer sheet. Then write the essay as described in Your Task. You may use scrap paper to take notes as you read and to plan your written response.

Your Task:

> After you have read the passages and answered the multiple-choice questions, write a unified essay in which you compare the attitudes of Williams and Franklin with regard to how European colonists should treat the Native Americans. In your essay, use ideas from both passages to develop your thesis. Using evidence from each passage, show how specific literary elements and techniques are used to convey the attitudes expressed in the selections.

Guidelines:

Be sure to

- Discuss the views of the proper treatment of Native Americans by colonists expressed in or implied by the selections

- Show how specific literary elements (e.g., theme, irony, and characterization) and specific techniques (e.g., satire) help to convey the attitudes expressed in each selection

- Organize your ideas in a unified and coherent manner

- Follow the conventions of standard written English

Boast Not, Proud English

by Roger Williams

[Editor's Note: Roger Williams (1603(?)–1683) was an English Puritan clergyman who emigrated to the Americas in 1631. Williams soon ran afoul of authorities in Massachusetts because of his support for religious freedom and his insistence that colonists could not simply take land from Native Americans but were required to purchase it. Most famous as the founder of Rhode Island and the Providence Plantations, Williams is also known for his pioneering work as a student of Native American language.]

Boast not, proud English, of thy birth and blood:
    Thy brother Indian is by birth as good.
Of one blood God made him, and thee, and all.
    As wise, as fair, as strong, as personal.
By nature, wrath's his portion, thine, no more
    Till Grace his soul and thine in Christ restore.
Make sure thy second birth, or thou shalt see
    Heaven ope¹ to Indians wild, but shut to thee.

---

¹ ope. Open

from
Remarks Concerning the Natives of North America
by Benjamin Franklin

The Indian men, when young, are hunters and warriors; when old, counselors; for all their government is by counsel of the sages. There is no force. There are no prisons, no officers to compel obedience or inflict punishment. Hence they generally study oratory, the best speaker having the most influence. The Indian women till the ground, dress the food, nurse and bring up the children, and preserve and hand down to posterity the memory of public transactions. These employments of men and women are accounted natural and honorable. Having few artificial wants, they have abundance of leisure for improvement by conversation. Our laborious manner of life, compared with theirs, they esteem slavish and base, and the learning on which we value ourselves they regard as frivolous and useless.

An instance of this occurred at the Treaty of Lancaster, in Pennsylvania, anno 1744, between the government of Virginia and the Six Nations [of the Iroquois Confederacy]. After the principal business was settled, the commissioners from Virginia acquainted the Indians by a speech that there was at Williamsburg a college with a fund for educating Indian youth, and that, if the Six Nations would send down half a dozen of their young lads to that college, the government would take care that they should be well provided for and instructed in all the learning of the white people.

It is one of the Indian rules of politeness not to answer a public proposition the same day that it is made. They think it would be treating it as a light matter and that they show it respect by taking time to consider it, as of a matter important. They therefore deferred their answer till the day following; when their speaker began, by expressing their deep sense of the kindness of the Virginia government in making them that offer:

"For we know," says he, "that you highly esteem the kind of learning taught in those Colleges, and that the maintenance of our young men, while with you, would be very expensive to you. We are convinced, therefore, that you mean to do us good by your proposal, and we thank you heartily. But you, who are wise, must know that different nations have different conceptions of things; and you will therefore not take it amiss if our ideas of this kind of education happen not to be the same with yours. We have had some experience of it. Several of our young people were formerly brought up at the colleges of the northern provinces. They were instructed in all your sciences, but when they came back to us, they were bad runners, ignorant of every means of living in the woods, unable to bear either cold or hunger, knew neither how to build a cabin, take a deer, or kill an enemy, spoke our language imperfectly, were therefore neither fit for hunters, warriors, nor counselors. They were totally good for nothing. We are, however, not the less obliged by your kind offer, though we decline accepting it. And to show our grateful sense of it, if the gentlemen of Virginia will send us a dozen of their sons, we will take great care of their education, instruct them in all we know, and make men of them."

The Iroquois False Face Society was a healing group that utilized grotesque wooden masks to frighten evil spirits believed to cause illness.

Multiple-Choice Questions

Directions: Select the best suggested answer to each question and write its letter on your answer sheet. The questions may help you think about ideas and information that you might want to use in your writing. You may return to these questions any time you wish.

1. **The line "As wise, as fair, as strong, as personal" is an example of**
   (a) parallelism.
   (b) metaphor.
   (c) simile.
   (d) irony.

2. **The poem "Boast Not, Proud English" is addressed to**
   (a) Native Americans.
   (b) English people who think that they are better than the Native Americans.
   (c) English people who consider the Native Americans their brothers.
   (d) members of the Puritan church.

3. **The repetition of *b* sounds in *birth*, *blood*, and *brother* is an example of**
   (a) onomatopoeia.
   (b) simile.
   (c) alliteration.
   (d) rhythm.

4. **According to the speaker of Williams's poem, if the English person is not reborn, then he will find that heaven is**
   (a) open to him and closed to Native Americans.
   (b) closed to him but open to Native Americans.
   (c) closed to all.
   (d) open to all.

5. **With which statement would the speaker of "Boast Not, Proud English" agree?**
   (a) English people are better than Native Americans.
   (b) Native Americans are better than English people.
   (c) English people are no better and no worse than Native Americans.
   (d) English people can go to heaven, but Native Americans cannot.

6. **According to Franklin's essay, the commissioners from Virginia offered to**
   (a) educate some Iroquois youth at the colonists' colleges.
   (b) buy the land belonging to the Iroquois.
   (c) send their youth to be educated among the Iroquois.
   (d) join with the Iroquois in a war against the French.

7. **The commissioners from Virginia believe that their educational system is superior. Therefore, the reply given to their offer is an example of**
   (a) metaphor.
   (b) simile.
   (c) allegory.
   (d) irony.

8. **To illustrate the theme that different peoples have different customs and are no better or worse than other peoples, Franklin**
   - (a) recites a narrative poem.
   - (b) shares an anecdote.
   - (c) writes a speech.
   - (d) relates a legend.

9. **The Iroquois spokesperson demonstrates the absurdity and pomposity of the Virginian's offer by**
   - (a) getting angry.
   - (b) refusing to respond immediately to the offer.
   - (c) making the same offer to the Virginians as they made to the Iroquois.
   - (d) laughing at the Virginians.

10. **According to Franklin, the Native Americans consider the colonists' manner of life**
    - (a) admirable and worthy of imitation.
    - (b) slavish and base.
    - (c) interesting but not for them.
    - (d) comical.

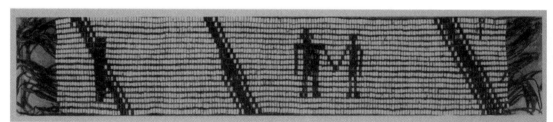

An Iroquois wampum belt

Part 4: Reading and Writing for Critical Analysis and Evaluation

Your Task:

Write a critical essay in which you discuss **two** works of literature you have read from the particular perspective of the statement that is provided for you in the **Critical Lens.** In your essay, provide a valid interpretation of the statement, agree **or** disagree with the statement as you have interpreted it, and support your opinion using specific references to appropriate literary elements from the two works. You may use scrap paper to plan your response.

Critical Lens:

> Literature is "at bottom a criticism of life."
> —Victorian poet and literary critic Matthew Arnold

Guidelines:

Be sure to

- Provide a valid interpretation of the Critical Lens that clearly establishes the criteria for analysis
- State whether you agree or disagree with Matthew Arnold's view of literature
- Select two works you have read that you believe best support your opinion
- Use the criteria suggested by the Critical Lens to analyze the works you have chosen
- Avoid plot summary. Instead, use specific references to appropriate literary elements (e.g., plot, setting, characterization, tone, theme, figurative language) to show how the works you have chosen support your opinion about the Critical Lens statement
- Organize your ideas in a unified and coherent manner
- Follow the conventions of standard written English
- Specify the titles and authors of the literature you use

HIGH SCHOOL

COMPREHENSIVE EXAMINATION

IN

ENGLISH

PART ___

ANSWER SHEET

Student_____ Grade_____

School_____ Teacher_____

**Write your answers for the multiple-choice questions for Part __
on this answer sheet.**

Part ___

1. _____   6. _____

2. _____   7. _____

3. _____   8. _____

4. _____   9. _____

5. _____   10. _____

   I do hereby affirm, at the close of this examination, that I had no unlawful knowledge of the questions or answers prior to the examination and that I have neither given nor received assistance in answering any of the questions during the examination.

_____
Signature

Use the following checklist to proofread the compositions that you write for lessons in this book.

Spelling	○ Is every word in the composition spelled correctly? ○ Are all names and titles spelled correctly?
Grammar	○ Does each verb agree in number with its subject? ○ Have you avoided split infinitives? ○ Are verb tenses consistent and correct? ○ Are irregular verb forms used correctly? ○ Have you used the present tense when describing action in a literary work? ○ Is the referent of every pronoun clear? ○ Do pronouns agree with their antecedents? ○ Have you avoided sentence fragments? ○ Have you avoided run-on sentences? ○ Have you avoided double negatives? ○ Have you avoided dangling or misplaced modifiers? ○ Have you used the right cases of pronouns such as *I* and *me*, *who* and *whom*?
Usage	○ Have frequently confused words, such as *lie* and *lay*, *then* and *than*, *effect* and *affect*, *too* and *to*, *principle* and *principal*, *it's* and *its*, *their* and *there*, *between* and *among*, been used correctly?
Mechanics	○ Does every sentence end with an appropriate end mark? ○ Have you used commas, semicolons, hyphens, dashes, and ellipsis marks correctly? ○ Does every direct quotation have quotation marks around it? ○ Have you capitalized the first word of each sentence and all proper nouns and adjectives? ○ Have you used quotation marks around the titles of short works such as short stories or poems and underlined the titles of long works such as plays or novels?
Manuscript Form	○ Have you double-spaced your manuscript? ○ Have you indented your paragraphs? ○ Have you centered your title and used quotation marks around it? ○ Have you used ample margins? ○ Have you written neatly? Is every word legible?

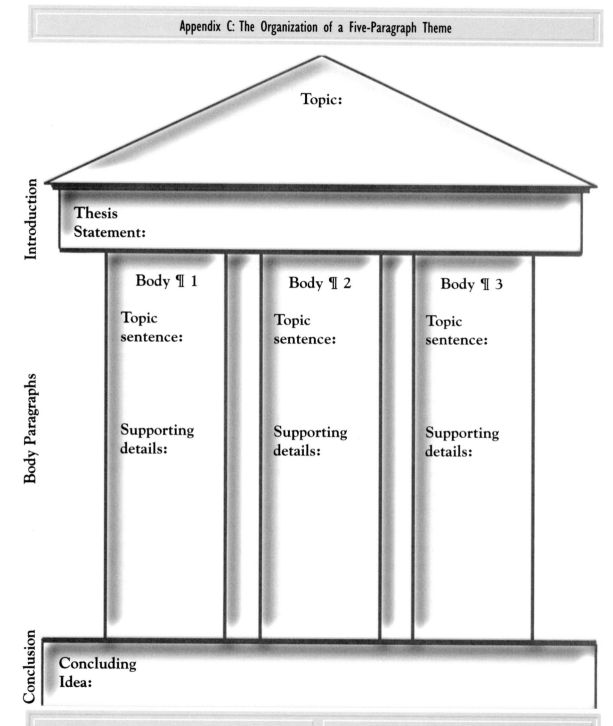

The following are words commonly misspelled by students in essay examinations. Practice several of these words each day until you are certain that you can spell each of them correctly.

A

absence
absolutely
accidentally
accommodate
achievement
acknowledge
acquaintance
adequate
again
always
ambiguous
among
analysis
ancestor
announcement
answer
anticipate
antique
anxious
apology
apparently
approximately
arguing
argument
article
artificial
asked
assessment
assistance
audience
average

B

beautiful
beggar
been
beginning
believe
biased
break
brilliance
business

C

calendar
candidate
can't
career
ceiling
certainly
challenge
changeable
choose
coming
commitment
committee
committing
comparable
comparative
comparison
competent
competition
competitor
conceive

concentrate
conference
conscience
conscious
consequently
continuous
convenience
could
courageous
criticism
criticize
cruelty
curiosity

D

dear
debt
deceitful
defense
definite
despise
devise
dialogue
dictionary
disappear
discouragement
disillusioned
disloyal
dissatisfied
does
done
dramatize

E

eighth
elaborate
eliminate
embarrass
emphasis
encourage
enormous
enough
entrance
environment
essential
exaggerate
exceed
excellent
excessively
excitement
existence
explanation
extraordinary

F

familiarize
fascinate
feasible
February
fickle
fierce
figuratively
finally
flexible
foremost

foreshadow
foreword
fortunately
forty
forward
friend

G

gauge
genre
gracious
grammar
grateful
guarantee
guess
guest

H

half
having
hear
height
heir
here
heritage
heroes
heroine
hoarse
humorous
hypocrisy

I

identity
illness

imagination
imitate
immature
immediately
inadequate
inconceivable
incredible
independence
individual
influential
information
initiative
instead
integrity
intelligence
intention
interpretation
intriguing
irresistible
irresponsible

J

journal
journey
just
juvenile

K

knew

L

legend
license
literally

loneliness
loose
lose
loveliness
loyalty

M

magnificent
maintain
maintenance
making
maneuver
many
marriage
masterpiece
meant
medieval
metaphor
minimum
minute
mischievous
misinterpret
misspell
misunderstood
monologue
moral
morale
morality

N

narrative
negative
neighbor
neither

nineteenth
ninety
none
nonsense
noticeable
nuisance

O

obnoxious
obstacle
occasion
occurrence
offense
often
once
opinion
opportunity
optimistic
ordinary
organization
original
outrageous

P

pamphlet
paradoxical
parallel
partially
peculiar
performance
permanent
physical
piece
piercing

playwright
possess
possessive
practical
prairie
preceding
precious
preface
preferred
prejudice
pretense
prevalent
primarily
privilege
proceed
prominent
propaganda
publicity

Q
quiet
quite

R
raise
read
ready
rearrange
reciprocate
recommendation
recurring
regardless
regretted
relief
repetitious

resemblance
resolution
responsible
rewriting
rhyme
rhythm
ridiculous
routine

S
sacrifice
safely
safety
said
sarcastic
says
scenery
seems
seize
separate
separation
sequence
similar
simile
since
sincerity
skillful
softening
sophisticated
specific
spectacle
spectacular
statistics
straight
studying

successful
superb
supersede
sure
surprising
syllable
symbol
symbolize
synonym

T
temporary
their
there
they
thinness
thorough
though
through
tonight
too
tragedy
tragic
transferred
transparent
treachery
tremendous
truly
Tuesday
twelfth
two

U
unbearable
unconscious

uncontrollable
used
usually

V
valuable
various
viewpoint
villain
visualize

W
warrior
weather
Wednesday
weight
weird
where
whether
which
whole
wield
witnesses
woman
women
won't
would
write
writing
wrote

Y
yield

analyze, v. To break something into its parts, describe the parts, and show how the parts are related to each other and to the whole

argument, n. Writing or speech that puts forward reasons in support of an opinion or factual proposition

assess, v. To determine the value of something

assessment, n. A judgment. See *judgment.*

categorize, v. To put items into categories; to classify them

cause, n. That which produces an effect, result, or consequence

chart, n. Any of a number of different kinds of informative graphic materials, such as a table, illustration, or graph

cite, v. To refer to or mention as an example or proof

coherent, adj. Said of a piece of writing in which the ideas are logically connected and in a sensible order. To make a piece of writing coherent, one organizes the ideas and uses transitions to connect them.

compare, v. To show the similarities between two subjects

contrast, v. To explain the differences between two subjects

conventions, n. Agreed-upon regularities in writing, including the rules for spelling, grammar, usage, punctuation, capitalization, and manuscript form

convey, v. Literally, to carry; figuratively, to show or illustrate to someone else

criterion, n. A standard, rule, test, or benchmark on which a decision or judgment is based. For example, one might choose a college based on the criterion of cost or based on the criterion of size. Plural: *criteria.*

Critical Lens, n. phrase. On the Comprehensive Examination, a term used to describe a statement that expresses a viewpoint from which literature can be interpreted or judged

critique, v. To perform a critical analysis of a work or an idea

describe, v. To tell about something in detail, to give a detailed verbal account of something

effect, n. The result or consequence of something. For example, the images and events in a horror story might have the effect of creating suspense.

evaluate, v. To judge the merits and demerits of something

evidence, n. Facts given in support of an opinion or argument. In essays about literary works, the evidence is information from the literary works, including quotations, paraphrases, summaries, and descriptions of literary elements and techniques.

excerpt, n. A part of a longer work. For example, one might select a single anecdote, or very short story told to make a point, from an autobiography or biography. Such a selection would be an excerpt.

explain, v. To tell why or how something is the way it is

express, v. To make a statement that reveals thoughts or feelings

expression, n. A statement or part of a statement

generalization, n. A statement that refers to many specific instances or particulars or to all of something

generalize, n. To make a statement that refers to many specific instances or to all of something

graph, n. A drawing that shows relationships between variables, such as a bar graph, line graph, or pie chart

graphic, n. Any item, such as a graph, map, or diagram, that presents information visually

illustrate, v. To give an example

inference, n. A conclusion that can be drawn from a set of facts

interpret, v. To explain or describe the meaning or significance of something, such as a painting or a poem

interpretation, n. An explanation of the meaning or significance of a work of art, based upon careful study of the work and attention to its details and techniques

judgment, n. An opinion as to the value or worth of something; an evaluation or assessment

key idea, n. phrase. A part of a piece of writing that is central to its meaning; an important or crucial point

literary element, n. phrase. A part of a literary work, such as its plot, setting, mood, or theme

literary technique, n. phrase. A special device used in a literary work. There are literary techniques related to meaning, such as metaphors and similes; literary techniques related to sound, such as alliteration and onomatopoeia; and literary techniques related to structure, such as the surprise ending or the beginning *in media res* (in the middle of the action).

logical, adj. Based upon sound reasons and arguments; supported by facts and by the relationships among the facts

main idea, n. phrase. The most important, key, or central idea in a piece of writing, also known as the thesis or the controlling idea

objective, adj. Based upon fact, not opinion; provable by reference to the facts or evidence

opinion, n. A judgment, belief, prediction, or other statement that cannot be proved, absolutely, by observation but that can, if the opinion is sound, be supported by facts

organization, n. The arrangement of ideas in a piece of writing

organize, v. To arrange ideas so that they follow logically from one to another and so the relationships among the ideas are clear to the reader. Common ways of organizing writing include chronological order, order of importance, and spatial order.

paraphrase, *n.* A restatement in other words

passage, *n.* A short selection from a piece of writing, ranging in size from a couple of sentences to a few paragraphs

proposition, *n.* A statement of fact that can be proved by definition, by observation, or by consulting an authoritative expert or reference work

recommendation, *n.* An opinion as to what someone else should do or think, usually based on specific facts or evidence presented in support of the opinion

relationship, *n.* A connection or association between two people, things, or ideas

relevant, *adj.* Related to the matter or issue being discussed; pertinent

response, *n.* A reaction to something. For example, an essay might be a response to an essay question.

review, *v.* To examine something carefully and make a judgment about it based on the examination

selection, *n.* A part of a literary work or other piece of writing

show, *v.* To give evidence

specific, *n.* Particular, not vague or general. When an essay prompt asks you to be specific, you are being asked to give precise, detailed facts or evidence in your answer.

statement, *n.* Any short, meaningful writing or speech, such as a sentence, opinion, proposition, etc.

structure, *n.* The form and organization of a piece of writing. For example, an essay might have a five-paragraph structure, consisting of an introduction, three body paragraphs, and a conclusion. A short story might be structured as a series of flashbacks to an earlier time in a character's life.

subjective, *adj.* Based upon the opinions or internal, private experiences of an individual rather than upon observable facts that can be verified by others

summarize, *v.* To restate in fewer words

support, *v.* To provide evidence to back up an assertion (a statement of fact or an opinion). In a paragraph, the sentences in the body support the topic sentence. In an essay, the paragraphs of the body support the thesis statement, or controlling idea.

table, *n.* A kind of chart in which information is presented in list form in columns and rows

unified, *adj.* A piece of writing is unified if its ideas are all related to a single controlling idea and all contribute to creating a single dominant impression on the reader.

allegory. A work in which many of the elements, such as the characters or the parts of the setting, symbolize, or represent, things beyond themselves

anecdote. A very brief story told to illustrate a point

article. An extended piece of nonfiction writing of the kind found in newspapers, magazines, and newsletters

autobiography. The story of a person's life, written by that person, a kind of nonfiction

ballad. A simple narrative poem in four-line stanzas, usually meant to be sung

biography. The story of a person's life, written by someone else, a kind of nonfiction

blank verse. Unrhymed poetry written in iambic pentameter

body. The part of an essay or composition in which ideas are presented to support the main idea presented in the introduction

character. A being who takes part in the action of a literary work

comedy. Originally referring to any literary work with a happy ending, this term is now used, primarily, of plays, screenplays, or other dramas that are light-hearted or humorous or in which the main character meets a pleasant fate.

conclusion. The final portion of an essay, often a single paragraph, in which the writer sums up his or her thoughts

conflict. Struggle in which the characters are involved. Conflict can be *internal* (inside a character) or *external* (with a person or force outside the character).

controlling idea. The single main idea that unifies a piece of writing. This term is generally considered to be synonymous with the term thesis statement, although some people make a distinction between a thesis statement, which simply presents a proposition, and a controlling idea, which also conveys the writer's purpose. For most practical purposes, the two terms may be considered synonyms.

criticism. The act of interpreting and/or evaluating a literary work

description. A type of writing that has as its purpose presenting a portrait, in words, of some subject

diary. See *journal.*

drama. Writing that presents events through the dialogue and, sometimes, the movements and actions, of characters. Types of drama include stage plays, screenplays, radio plays, and reader's theater. Drama may be read or performed by actors.

dramatic dialogue. A dramatic poem in which two characters speak

dramatic monologue. A dramatic poem in which one character speaks

dramatic poem. A verse that presents the speech of one or more characters in a dramatic situation

elegy. A formal poem about death or loss

epic. A long story, often in verse, involving heroes and gods and providing a portrait of a culture, of its legends, beliefs, values, laws, arts, and ways of life. Ex: the *Iliad,* the *Aeneid, Beowulf,* and *Paradise Lost.*

epistle. A letter, which may be in verse. A novel written in letters is known as an *epistolary novel.*

essay. A brief work of prose nonfiction. A good essay develops a single controlling idea and is characterized by unity and coherence.

expository writing. See *informative writing.*

expressive writing. Writing that has as its purpose describing personal feelings, attitudes, ideas, values, or beliefs. Personal essays are a kind of expressive writing.

fable. A brief story with animal characters told to illustrate a moral

fantasy. A literary work that contains highly unrealistic elements, such as Swift's *Gulliver's Travels*

farce. A type of comedy, often satirical, that depends heavily on so-called low humor and on improbable, wildly exaggerated characters and situations

fiction. A literary work, in prose, that tells about imaginary people, places, and events. Examples of fiction include short stories, novellas, and novels.

flashback. A section of a literary work that presents an event or series of events that occurred earlier than the current time in the work

folk tale. A brief story passed by word of mouth from generation to generation

free verse. Poetry that avoids the use of regular rhyme, rhythm, meter, or division into stanzas

genre. One of the types or categories into which literary works are divided

image. A word or phrase that names something that can be seen, heard, touched, tasted, or smelled

imagery. The collective images used in a work

informative writing. Writing that has as its purpose teaching the reader about a subject. Informative writing, also known as expository writing, presents facts, not opinions.

introduction. The opening part of a piece of writing. In a nonfiction essay, the introduction should grab the attention of the reader and present the subject and main idea, or thesis. In a short story, the introduction generally presents the setting, provides necessary background information, and introduces the protagonist and the central conflict.

irony. A contradiction, such as a difference between appearance and reality or a difference between what is said and what is meant

journal. A day-to-day account of events; a diary. Such an account may be true (nonfiction) or imaginary (fiction).

legend. A story, which may be partially or wholly true, about a hero or heroine. Stories about the exploits of King Arthur and Annie Oakley are examples of legends.

lyric poem. A short, highly musical verse that expresses the thoughts and emotions of a speaker

Magical Realist fiction. Fiction that contains both realistic and fantastic elements, intermingled

melodrama. A drama containing exaggerated characters and events characterized by excessive and often sentimental emotion

memoir. An account of events from the past, told by someone who took part in those events; a synonym, with slightly different connotations, of the term *autobiography*

mood. The emotional quality evoked by a literary work

motivation. A force, object, or circumstance that impels a character to act as he or she does; the act of being impelled to think or do something

motive. A reason why a character acts as he or she does

myth. A story dealing with a god or goddess or with supernatural occurrences. Often myths explain the origins of natural phenomena. The Greek story of Prometheus the fire-giver is an example.

narrative. Any work of prose, poetry, or drama, fictional or nonfictional, that tells a story

narrative poem. A verse that tells a story

Naturalist fiction. Fiction that presents characters as subject to biological or natural forces beyond their power to control

nonfiction. Any of a wide variety of literary works, generally in prose, that present factual information or that present actual people, places, and events. Examples of nonfiction include speeches, essays, memoirs, autobiographies, biographies, textbooks, and reference works.

nonsense verse. A kind of light verse that contains elements that are silly, absurd, or meaningless

novel. A long work of prose fiction

novella. A short novel or long short story

parody. A literary work that imitates another work for humorous, often satirical purposes

periodical. A magazine, newsletter, or other publication that appears on a regular basis (e.g., monthly or quarterly)

personal essay. A short nonfiction work about a single topic that is autobiographical or biographical in nature or that expresses a subjective, personal view of a subject

persuasive writing. Writing that has as its purpose convincing others to adopt some belief or to take some action. Persuasive writing presents opinions.

position paper. An essay in which the writer presents his or her position, or opinion, with regard to some issue and backs up that opinion with factual evidence and/or persuasive rhetoric

prologue. An introduction to a literary work

proverb. A short, memorable statement that is passed by word of mouth from person to person, usually over many generations. "You can lead a horse to water, but you can't make it drink" is an example of a proverb.

psychological fiction. Fiction that emphasizes the subjective, interior experiences of characters; often fiction that deals with emotional or mental anguish or disturbance

purpose. The aim, or goal, of a piece of writing. Common purposes for writing include to inform, to persuade, to describe, to compare, to contrast, to define, to classify, to express personal thoughts or feelings, and to make a proposal or recommendation.

Realist fiction. Fiction that attempts to present an accurate, often critical, portrayal or imitation of reality

review. A type of nonfiction essay in which a critic presents an interpretation and evaluation of a work or group of works such as plays, movies, novels, concerts, or exhibitions of paintings

romance. 1. A medieval story about the adventures and loves of knights; 2. novels and other works involving exotic locales and extraordinary or mysterious events and characters; 3. nonrealistic fictions in general; 4. love stories

satire. A humorous literary work, in prose or in poetry, in which a writer pokes fun at something in order to point out errors, falsehoods, foibles, or failings

screenplay. A drama for film, television, or video

setting. The time and place in which a work of literature occurs

short story. A brief fictional work dealing with a central conflict and creating a single dominant impression

stage play. A kind of drama, consisting of stage directions and dialogue, that is performed on a stage by actors who portray characters

stanza. A recurring pattern of grouped lines in a poem

subplot. A subordinate story told in addition to the main story in a work of fiction

summary. A restatement, in other, fewer words

suspense. A feeling of curiosity, expectation, or anxiety created in the reader by questions about the outcome of the events in a literary work

tall tale. A story containing wildly exaggerated characters and events, like the stories about Paul Bunyan and Pecos Bill

theme. A central idea in a literary work. Often the theme is a lesson learned by the protagonist.

thesis statement. A statement of the main idea of an essay. The thesis statement appears in the introduction and may be a single sentence or more than one sentence.

tragedy. A type of drama in which the main character falls from a high to a low estate due to some failing, or weakness, known as a tragic flaw. The term is sometimes used, as well, of other types of literary work in which the main character meets a negative fate.

transition. Any word or phrase used to relate one idea or group of ideas in a piece of writing to other ideas or groups of ideas. Transitions, such as *first, next, however, in fact, as a result,* and *in conclusion,* help to bind a work together and to give it coherence.

Reading for Pretest, Part 1, page 22

"The Birth of the Net," from *The Complete Student's Guide to the Internet,* by Allyson Stanford

The Internet is a vast system of computers, scattered around the world, that are connected to one another in one gigantic network. Another name for the Internet, given to it by Al Gore, is the Information Superhighway. Computers can be hooked up to the Internet by means of ordinary telephone lines, by cables like those used by cable television, or by wireless connections, which make use of signals that travel through the air.

Almost any computer can be connected to the Internet, from the large mainframe computers and powerful workstation computers used by universities and corporations to the small personal computers and laptops used by individuals. Most people connect to the Internet from personal computers using ordinary telephone lines and special pieces of hardware known as modems.

The Internet began as a special network created by the United States government to connect researchers and officials working on projects for the Department of Defense. In 1955, President Dwight D. Eisenhower created the Advanced Research Projects Agency, also known as ARPA, to fund and coordinate defense-related scientific projects in the United States. In 1969, the Advanced Research Projects Agency created a network known as the ARPANet to connect computers at the Defense Department to computers at research centers and universities around the country. The ARPANet used high-speed transmission lines to connect computers at the University of California at Los Angeles, the University of California at Santa Barbara, the Stanford Research Institute, and the University of Utah in Salt Lake City. In the years that followed, the ARPANet merged with other networks used to connect the Department of Defense with laboratories around the world, such as the European Center for Nuclear Research, Lawrence Livermore Laboratories, the Argon National Laboratory, and Los Alamos. This early version of the Internet was used almost exclusively by scientists—physicists and rocket scientists, for example—to exchange information related to defense projects such as building and testing new missiles.

The early Internet was almost completely text based. In other words, those scientists could use it to send words and numbers, but not sounds, pictures, video, and the like. By the early 1980s, people were starting to use the term Internet to describe the system of connected defense and research computers.

What makes the Internet different from previous networks is that every computer on the Internet is connected to every other computer instead of being connected to one gigantic computer at a central location. The Department of Defense gave the Internet this kind of peer-to-peer organization because they were worried about what might happen to a centralized supercomputer in the case of a nuclear war. In such a war, if the enemy bombed the central computer, then the whole system would go down. By using a peer-to-peer organization, the Department of Defense made sure that even if some computers and their connections were destroyed, the others would still be able to send and receive messages. So, the Internet, with its ability to send and receive messages from any computer on the network to any other computer on the network, was an outgrowth of the Cold War.

The most important event in the history of the Internet occurred in 1979. In that year, Dr. Tim Berners-Lee of the European Center for Nuclear Research, also known as CERN, came up with the idea for the World Wide Web, which is one part of the Internet. The basic idea for the Web is simple. People create pages and store these on special computers known as servers. Each server and each page has its own unique address on the network. When a person creates a page for the World Wide Web, that page can contain links to any other page stored elsewhere in the world on a computer connected to the Internet. In other words, the World Wide Web is a system of pages, stored on computers around the world, that are connected to each other by links. By using a mouse to click on a link, you can instantly go to a page stored on a computer across the state, the country, or the world.

The wonderful thing about the World Wide Web is that pages can contain not only text but also sound, pictures, and movies. Anyone with a computer hooked up to the Internet can create a World Wide Web page and link it to other pages.

Because of Tim Berners-Lee's creation of the World Wide Web, the Internet has grown tremendously in the past few years. What started out to be a network for connecting a few scientists is now the Internet, connecting over 100 million users worldwide. By the year 2000, the number of people connected to the Internet is expected to grow to over 300 million. Soon, the entire world will be connected, and when that happens, the differences between the haves and the have-nots will dwindle.

The Internet has grown so rapidly because people can use it for many, many different purposes. They can go onto the World Wide Web to do research; to shop; to pay bills; to send electronic mail, or e-mail, to their friends; to talk to other people in electronic chat rooms; or just to entertain themselves. Whatever people are interested in—sports, books, music, movies, clothes, politics, just about anything—can be found today on the part of the Internet known as the World Wide Web.

Readings for Lesson 1.4, Activity B, page 41

"Careers for Art Students," by Ellen Best

My sister, Penelope, is a student in art school. She asked my advice about which career she should prepare for: elementary school art teacher or graphic designer. I asked her to tell me about both careers, so I could help her decide. It is equally easy to prepare for either job in her college, but she needs to choose.

Graphic designers help companies or institutions by designing the materials they present to the outside world. A graphic designer might design ads for the clients of an advertising agency, packaging for a soup company, books for a publisher, or posters for a library. Most graphic designers currently work with computer design tools. Although they may consult with a team to discuss what the product is trying to project, they usually do most of their work alone. Graphic design generally pays more money than most other career fields for artists. Graphic designers need to be able to create pleasing or innovative designs. They also need to be able to figure out what clients want. Graphic designers need to keep up with contemporary movements in design and with the latest technology.

An elementary school art teacher usually works for a school, teaching students how to work with various materials and methods to make art. Most art teachers work with the traditional handheld art media, like paint, clay, paper, ink, and scissors. They meet with several classes of twenty-five to thirty children every day. One good thing about this career is the schedule. If you can live on the modest salary, you can have several weeks during school vacations and ten weeks in the summer to do your own art projects. Elementary art teachers need to able to talk to and listen to children. They need to know what children can do at different levels of development. They need to be able to plan lessons, organize projects, purchase materials, and manage small budgets. Art teachers also need to keep up with new ideas in education.

from *All the Pretty Little Ponies,* by Jo Dignee

Mr. Akemi jumps out from behind the pyramid of soup cans. Kassandra gives a little gasp of shock, then starts to dust the boxes of chocolates that I bet are left over from last Valentine's Day. Valentine's Day 1950, maybe. He appears so suddenly I'd say he was hiding behind the soup, spying on us, waiting to catch us doing something wrong.

"What are you doing with that?" he demands, pointing to my notebook. "What are you writing in there?"

"I'm taking down Kassandra's home telephone number, Mr. Akemi," I say.

Akemi's eyes almost bulge from their sockets. His nostrils flare, and he gasps for breath. I wonder if he is really going to have a heart attack this time.

"Is that why I pay you, to make romance?" he shouts.

My toes curl with embarrassment. Kassandra edges toward the canned fruits, the beads on the ends of all her little braids clicking as she hurries.

"I'm taking the home number of all the clerks, so I can call around to find someone to cover, if anyone gets sick or something," I say.

"Lemme see," Akemi says, grabbing the notebook out of my hands. I stand there disgusted as he studies the list of names and numbers.

He looks me over—a long, silent appraisal from his small, shrewd eyes. "Mebbe you think I leave you this place after I die, make you rich," he says. Then he walks away, laughing.

Akemi. The weird thing is, despite his paranoia and suspicion and all, a lot of the time he's on to something. Maybe the whole list idea *was* just an excuse to get Kassandra's number.

Reading for Lesson 1.4, Activity C, page 43

"A Talent for Turning It Around," by Yvonne Barett

As the fourth child in a family of five, Walt Disney shouldn't have had a lonely childhood, but his father's harshness drove his older brothers from home one by one. To comfort himself, Walt filled his empty hours with the creations of his own pen. These creations, meant to amuse the young man, soon proved to be amusing to others. Always on the lookout for opportunity, Disney put his talents to work early. It wasn't just talent, however, that allowed Disney to build the largest and most innovative entertainment enterprise in the world. Disney possessed a trait that often leads to achievement: he looked for ways to turn negative situations into positive ones.

At the age of eighteen, Walt tried to find work as a cartoonist. When he was turned down by the local newspaper, he decided to accept a graphic design job in advertising. With this experience, he was able to move to a position making animated cartoon advertisements that were shown in movie theaters. Inspired by the antics of Felix the Cat, a popular cartoon character, Disney hoped to use his cartooning talents in entertainment, not to sell products.

By the time he was twenty-one, Disney had opened his first studio, where he and a partner animated classic children's stories. The distributor who was supposed to place copies of his films in movie theaters went bankrupt, and Disney did not get to see his first creations on the screen. Disney was learning his craft, however, and discovering how to be an entrepreneur, or business owner. Like many talented young people of his time, Walt was drawn to Hollywood, the burgeoning new center of the film industry.

Disney intended to direct films. In Hollywood, however, he encountered a lot of closed doors. No one wanted to hire this unknown young man to direct films. So Walt did what he knew how to do: he went into business for himself. "When you can't get a job," Disney said, "you start your own business." Working in his uncle's garage, Walt and his brother Roy started their Disney Brothers animation studio. Their first project was *Alice's Adventures.* An animated film based on *Alice in Wonderland*, this film incorporated a live actor playing Alice into an animated world. A distributor ordered six Alice films, at $1500 each. Disney's studio was in business.

Disney, who would go on to invent the most famous animated characters of all time, started off with a rabbit, not a mouse. He wanted to create a popular character, like Felix, who would star in a series of short films. He came up with Oswald the Lucky Rabbit, who did in fact become a popular "star." Unfortunately, Disney had signed a contract that gave ownership of the character to his distributor. In New York, where Walt had gone to sign his new contract, the distributor told the young man that his services were no longer needed. He told Walt that the distribution company owned the rights to Oswald. Walt swore then and there that he would never work for anyone else again.

Disney knew that if he didn't do something fast his studio would fail. On the train ride back to California, he came up with the idea of developing a mouse character. Mice overran his studio at night, and Walt was in the habit of capturing them and keeping them in cages on his desk. One mouse, he said, had become a special friend. The rest, of course, is history.

Reading for Posttest, Part 1, page 66

Excerpt from *They Fought for Freedom*, by Dale Berger

Who was the greatest American of all time? My personal candidate for this honor would be the Reverend Dr. Martin Luther King, Jr. I make this claim about Dr. King because I believe that he, above all others, understood that the ideals of equality on which our nation were founded must be more than simply ideals. They must be translated into practical realities. Dr.

King gave his life in the struggle to make the promise of the Declaration of Independence, the promise of "life, liberty, and the pursuit of happiness," a reality for every citizen, regardless of race, creed, or ethnic origin.

Martin Luther King, Jr., was born in Atlanta, Georgia, on January 15, 1929. King came by his interest in civil rights naturally. His grandfather had been a founder of the Atlanta chapter of the NAACP (the National Association for the Advancement of Colored People). His father, the Reverend Martin Luther King, Sr., was pastor of the Ebenezer Baptist Church and became a civil rights leader.

At the time of Martin Luther King's birth, the United States was far from living up to the promise of the Declaration. In many states throughout the country, African Americans were denied voting rights. Schools, lunch counters, buses, and other public facilities were segregated. African Americans were often denied accommodations in hotels designated for whites only. Discrimination was openly practiced and was in some places sanctioned by law. King worked to change all that.

King attended Morehouse College and Crozier Theological Seminary. At the latter institution, he was both student body president and valedictorian.

In 1953, he married Coretta Scott King, and in 1955 he graduated with a Ph.D. in divinity from Boston University. After graduation, he took up duties as pastor of the Dexter Avenue Baptist Church in Montgomery, Alabama. It was there that he began the activities that were to make him the leader of the American Civil Rights Movement.

In December of 1955, an African-American woman named Rosa Parks refused to give up her seat to a white man on a segregated bus in Montgomery and was arrested. Shortly thereafter, Dr. King began a boycott of the Montgomery bus system. King's house was bombed, and King and others were indicted under a state law prohibiting boycotts. Nonetheless, the boycott continued, and in 1956, after the Supreme Court declared Alabama's segregation laws unconstitutional, the Montgomery Transit Authority gave in and ended segregation of the buses. King had proved that peaceful, non-violent protest could be an effective agent of change.

King learned his political strategy, which is known as civil disobedience, from Mohandas K. Gandhi. Gandhi was a Hindu leader who won India's independence from Great Britain by means of peaceful, nonviolent protests,

including marches, boycotts, and sit-ins. Like that other great man of peace, Gandhi, Dr. King believed fervently that civil disobedience could be used as an effective weapon against oppression. As Dr. King wrote in his famous "Letter from the Birmingham Jail," in April of 1963, "Nonviolent direct action seeks to create such a crisis and establish such creative tension that a community that has constantly refused to negotiate is forced to confront the issue."

In 1957, King and other African-American ministers founded the Southern Christian Leadership Conference, or SCLC, which was to play an important role in securing civil rights for all Americans. In 1959, King returned to Atlanta, the headquarters of the SCLC, to assist his father at the Ebenezer Baptist Church and to work for civil rights. In the spring of 1963, after mass demonstrations in Birmingham, Alabama, led by Dr. King, President Kennedy reacted with legislation that became the Civil Rights Act of 1964, which made discrimination based on race against the law. In August of 1963, Dr. King led his famous March on Washington and was joined by over 250,000 protesters demanding that such legislation be passed. Standing in front of the

Lincoln Memorial, Dr. King gave his famous "I Have a Dream" speech in which he said:

"I have a dream that one day this nation will rise up and live out the true meaning of its creed—we hold these truths to be self-evident, that all men are created equal...

"I have a dream that one day on the red hills of Georgia the sons of former slaves and the sons of former slave owners will be able to sit down together at the table of brotherhood...

"I have a dream that my four little children will one day live in a nation where they will not be judged by the color of their skin but by the content of their character."

The following year, in 1964, President Johnson signed the Civil Rights Act into law. King was made *Time* magazine's Man of the Year and, in December, was awarded the Nobel Peace Prize.

In the years that followed, Dr. King continued to work tirelessly for civil rights. He drew criticism from some African-American leaders, such as Stokely Carmichael, for his insistence on civil disobedience, on using non-violent, peaceful means to effect change. He was investigated by F.B.I. director J. Edgar Hoover because of his opposition to the Vietnam War. King, however, stuck to his principles.

On April 4, 1968, this leader who had done so much to advance brotherhood and understanding was struck down by an assassin's bullet in Memphis, Tennessee, where he had gone to assist the cause of striking sanitation workers. Like Gandhi before him, this peaceful man, whose convictions had proved more powerful than all the forces of hate, nonetheless fell victim to an act of brutal, cowardly violence. It was a sad day for all who love liberty, but Dr. King's legacy will always be remembered. He proved the power of civil disobedience, and he brought about the most important piece of civil rights legislation that the world has ever known. These are real accomplishments, and no assassin's bullet could undo the great things that he had done.

Reading for Complete Practice Test, Part 1, page 192

"Pompeii: the Time Machine," by Robin Shulka

In A.D. 79, during the reign of the Roman emperor Titus, Pompeii was one of the most prosperous cities of Italy. Located just south of Naples, it was a busy, bustling seaport town, built in a rough circle about two miles in circumference and surrounded by a great wall with eight gates.

The inhabitants of Pompeii were very comfortable by the standards of the day. Taking advantage of their location on the southeastern Italian coast, the Pompeiians were able to carry on a flourishing trade with Rome, 125 miles to the north, and with various cities in the Mediterranean. Pompeii was known far and wide for its wines, oil, bread, millstones, fish sauces, perfumes, and cloth.

Within the city, the wealthy, urbane Pompeiians had built two theaters, a large amphitheater, a gymnasium for the training of its youth, many public fountains and baths, temples, and a forum. Pompeiians could entertain themselves at the theater, watch gladiatorial combats, bathe in luxury, and purchase goods from the shops of artisans, bakers, and wine merchants. Outside the city walls, on the green slopes of Mount Vesuvius, the Pompeiians grazed their goats and grew figs and olives.

Sixteen years before, in A.D. 63, the city had been shaken by an earthquake, but the citizens had quickly set about the task of rebuilding and had returned to their happy day-to-day lives. Then, suddenly, in August of A.D. 79, Vesuvius began to rumble, filling the sky with a light rain of ash. The Pompeiians must have been dismayed at this, but not so dismayed as to leave their homes. This proved to be a fatal mistake, for the volcano suddenly erupted, throwing a column of hot gas and ash at very high speed tens of thousands of feet into the sky. As much as a cubic mile of material was blown from the volcano at temperatures as high as 700° Fahrenheit. A deadly rain of superheated ash and stone traveling at over seventy miles an hour, far faster than a person can run, fell upon the city, burying it and killing thousands of people. From fifteen to twenty feet of tephra—ash, pumice, and other materials from the crater of the volcano—fell upon Pompeii, preserving it, for all time, as a record of the Roman way of life.

In 1748 the buried city of Pompeii was discovered, and shortly after that, archaeological excavations began. Today, most of the ancient city has been unearthed. The ash has been cleared away, and beneath the ash, almost perfectly preserved, are the homes, shops, public facilities, streets, walls, and other parts of this ancient Roman city. Walking down the streets of Pompeii today is an eerie experience, like being transported back two thousand years via a time machine. One can sit on a seat in an ancient Roman theater, see the jars in shops where people stored wine, see mosaics on the floors of people's homes, look into the baths, stare at the statues and frescoes on the walls—all as one might have done two thousand years ago.

Not only the buildings and the streets but also the very people and animals of ancient Pompeii have been preserved. By pouring plaster into the spaces left by the decayed bodies of the buried Pompeiians, archaeologists have created casts of those bodies, allowing us, today, to gaze on the faces of these ancient Romans, to see the very folds of their clothing and straps of their sandals. Today, thousands of tourists visit Pompeii every year to walk down the streets of this ancient city and to view the plaster casts of these ancient Romans. Many tourists also take the trip up the slopes of Vesuvius to gaze into the caldera—the boiling mouth—of the volcano.

Pompeii offers a unique opportunity to look into the past and see it as it actually was. It also offers a warning about the power of nature, a warning that modern people seem not to have heeded. There have been more than thirty eruptions of Vesuvius since A.D. 79, the most recent being in 1944. An eruption in 1631 killed around 3,500 people. Today, Vesuvius remains an active volcano. Another eruption of the magnitude of the one in A.D. 79 would destroy an area of about four square miles around the volcano. There are, today, nearly a million people living in the area that would be immediately affected by another eruption.

A

achievement tests, 4
alliteration, 130, 135
analysis chart, 39–40
analyzing, 39, 176–179
anecdote, 127
antagonist, 145
antithesis, 130
anxiety, 7–10
aptitude tests, 3
apostrophe, 129
audience, 16, 26, 64, 80, 106
autobiographies, 126
author, 180

B

bar graphs, 95, 101
biographical essays, 126
body paragraphs, 48, 49, 56–59, 65, 90, 107, 161, 184, 185, 209

C

capitalization, 69, 112, 165, 208
captions, 101
cause-and-effect chart, 37–38
central conflict, 145, 146
character, 128, 145
character analysis chart, 40

charts, 34–43, 101
chronological order, 26, 57
climax, 145
cluster chart, 38–39
coherence, 26, 80, 172
column graphs, 95–96, 101
comparing and contrasting, 157–159
comparison/contrast chart, 34–35
Comprehensive English Examination overview, 11–14
conclusions, 48–49, 60–63, 65, 107, 161, 185, 209
context clues, 8
controlling idea/purpose. See thesis statement.
conventions, 26, 80, 123, 173, 208
couplet, 131
crisis, 145
Critical Lens, 171–172, 184; analyzing, 176–179; samples, 178

D

dangling modifiers, 69
development, 123, 172
diagrams, 99
diary, 127
dramatic poetry, 127
dynamic character, 145

E

elaboration, 153
ellipsis, 155
end rhyme, 131
essay, example of, 49; planning body of, 157–159; writing 184–185. See also five-paragraph theme.
evidence, 86, 153, 173; from literature, 153, 161, 185
examination prompts, terms in, 212–213
examination tasks, 12
external conflict, 145

F

facts, 83–92
falling action, 145
fiction, 127
figurative language, 129
figures of speech, 129
first-person, 65, 107, 145
five-paragraph theme, 48, 209
flashback, 129
flat character, 145
foreshadowing, 129
form, 16, 64, 80, 106, 122, 172
free verse, 131

G

genres, 126–127, 180
grammar, 161, 165, 208
graphic organizers, 34–43, 65

H

heptastich, 131
hyperbole, 129

I

icons, 100
images, 128
inciting incident, 145
infographics, 93–105
informative writing, 48–51, 89–90
internal conflict, 145
internal rhyme, 131
introduction, 48–49, 52–55, 64, 160, 184, 209
irony, 129

J

journals, 126
judgments, 84

K

keys, 97, 100–101

L

labels, 101

legend, on map, 97, 101
line graphs, 93, 101
listening selections, 217–224
literary techniques, 135–136, 181
literary terms, 146, 214–216
literature, elements and techniques in, 126–132, 173; genres of, 126–132; list of recommended, 182; terms to describe, 214–216
logical organization, 26, 80, 89–90, 122
lyric poem, 127, 133–140

M

main character, 145
main idea, 29, 48, 89–90, 135
manuscript form, 208
maps, 99–100
mechanics, 208
memoirs, 126
metaphor, 129, 136
meter, 131
metrical verse, 131
minor character, 145
misplaced modifiers, 65, 69
mood, 128, 145, 181
motivation, 145
motive, 145

multiple-choice questions, 15–18, 44–45, 64, 160; sample answer sheet, 207
myths, 126

N

narrative poetry, 126, 127
narratives, 126, 141–152
narrator, 145
nonfiction, 127
notetaking, 29–33, 57, 64, 106, 181; on literature, 181; on narrative, 146–147, 160; on poem, 136–137; using graphic organizers, 34–40

O

octave, 131
onomatopoeia, 130
opinions, 83–92; reasonable vs. unreasonable, 84; supporting, 85–86; types of, 84–85
order of importance, 57, 80
organization, 26, 80, 89–90, 122, 172
outlining. See rough outline.

P

parallelism, 130

paraphrasing, 134, 153, 176
Part 1, Posttest, 66–67;
  Pretest, 21–24; summary
  of steps for, 64–65; tasks
  for, 12, 25; writing
  prompt for, 25–28
Part 2, Posttest, 108–112;
  Pretest, 73–78; summary
  of steps for, 106–107;
  tasks for, 12, 79; writing
  prompt for, 79–80
Part 3, Posttest, 162–166;
  Pretest for, 115–121;
  summary of steps for,
  160–161; tasks for, 12,
  122; writing prompt for,
  122–125
Part 4, Posttest, 188;
  preparing for, 180–183;
  Pretest, 169–170;
  summary of steps for,
  187; task for, 12
percentages, 97–98
personal essays, 126
personification, 129, 136
persuasive writing, 89–92
pie charts, 96–98, 101
plot, 99–100, 145, 181
poem, 127, 133–140
point of view, 145
position papers, 171–172,
  176
practice test, 189–206
predictions, 85

pro-and-con chart, 37
pronoun reference, 69, 208
proofreading, 65, 68–70,
  107, 161, 165; checklist
  for, 208; symbols for, 69,
  112, 165
protagonist, 145, 181
punctuation, 68, 161, 165,
  208
purpose, 16, 26, 64, 80,
  106, 122, 172

Q
quatrain, 131
quotations, 68, 146, 181;
  from literary works,
  153–155 ; guidelines for,
  154–155

R
reading for information,
  71–112
repetition, 130
resolution, 145
rhetorical question, 130
rhetorical techniques, 130
rhyme scheme, 131
rhymed verse, 131, 136
rhythm, 130
rising action, 145
rough outline, 29–33, 34,
  37, 65, 158, 160
run-ons, 69, 106–107

S
satire, 127
scale, of map, 100
Scholastic Aptitude Test
  (SAT), 4
sentence fragments, 69
sestet, 131
setting, 128, 145, 181
short stories, 126
simile, 129
slant rhyme, 131
sonnet, 131
source of information for
  writing, 16, 25, 79, 122,
  171
speaker, 134–135
spelling, 65, 107, 161, 173,
  208–209
standardized tests, 1–6
stanza, 131
stanza form, 131
statement of belief, 85
statement of obligation, 85
statement of policy, 85
statement of value, 85
static character, 145
stereotypical character, 145
stock character, 145
story map, 148–151
style, 129
subject, 128, 134, 146
summary, 146, 153
supporting details/ideas,
  204

suspense, 128
symbol, 129
synesthesia, 129

T

tables, 98, 101
tall tales, 127
techniques involving
  sound, 130
tercet, 131
test prompts, 15–18,
  25–28, 79–82, 122–125,
  171–174, 176–177
theme, 128, 146, 180; of
  poem, 135
thesis statement
  (controlling idea/purpose),
  48–49, 52–55, 65, 89–90,
  107, 160, 177, 209

third-person, 65, 107, 145
timeline, 36
titles, of graphics, 101;
  quotation marks vs.
  underlining for, 161
tone, 80, 106, 128, 145
topic sentences, 57, 90,
  107, 153, 185, 209
topic, 16, 25, 64, 79, 106,
  122, 160, 172
transitions, 26, 57, 58, 64,
  80, 107
triplet, 131
turning point, 145

U

understatement, 129
unified, 26, 80, 172
usage, 69, 161, 165, 208

V

variable, 93–101
Venn diagram, 35–36
verb agreement, 68
verbatim, 153
voice, 80, 106, 129

W

word web, 38–39
writing prompts, 15–18,
  22, 25–28, 79–82,
  171–175, 176–177

X

x-axis, 93–96

Y

y-axis, 93–96